An Oregon Legal Guides book

Using
Small Claims Court
in Oregon

Second Editon

Janay Haas, JD

Check www.oregonlegalguides.com for periodic updates.

This book is dedicated to Laura Orr

and John Van Landingham,

local heroes.

Acknowledgments

Thanks, great big ones, are due to those who offered guidance, support, and old-fashioned pointers in the development of this book. Without them, there would be no book. Among those people are Laura Orr, who applied significant moral pressure, peppered me with questions from patrons of the Washington County Law Library, and shared research and other resources on small claims procedure in Oregon; John van Landingham, an advocate for the rights of low-income Oregonians in numerous venues and the author of the booklet "Small Claims Court in Lane County," the primary source for this guide; lawyer and editor Mary Oberst, whose patient and gentle editorial skills made the book more readable; George Bock, retired owner of Caveman Credit in Grants Pass, who reviewed the whole manuscript and who commented substantially on the practical aspects of judgments and how to collect them; attorneys James Young of Coos Bay and Denise Harrington of Tillamook, who shared expertise on justice courts; and Washington County attorney Pamela Yee and the Hons. Thomas Ryan and Steve Todd, Multnomah County circuit court judges, who looked critically at the book with an eye toward how much it was going to help people on their own to arrive at a fair solution to their legal problems. I accepted many of the suggestions these kind and helpful people offered, and the book is better for them. I am the only one responsible for the accuracy, clarity, and comprehensiveness of the material in the book, of course.

TABLE OF CONTENTS

INTRODUCTION

Using Small Claims Court in Oregon

What this book does

If you're reading this, chances are you're looking for help in deciding what to do about a problem you've had with another person, or a business, or even a government agency. Or maybe you've just found out that someone is suing you in small claims court, and you want to know how to protect your interests on trial day.

This book is designed to guide you in making those decisions. It won't give you specific legal advice about your own situation, but it will:

- Tell you how small claims court works in Oregon,
- Help you look at the worth and the risks of your case,
- Give you pointers and strategies you may want to consider, and
- Alert you to some traps you will want to avoid.

After reading this book, you should be in a much better position to decide what you want to do about your situation, and how to do it.

What this book doesn't do

Unfortunately, no book can tailor its information so that it fits everyone's situation exactly. *This book is a source of information only; it cannot and does not give you legal advice.* The law is complex: a fact that seems unimportant can make a big difference in which law applies or how things work out. That's why it's important to get legal advice—from a lawyer, not a book—about your particular situation.

How to use this book

Whether you are the person who starts the case (the **plaintiff**) or the person who is forced to respond to a case filed against you (the **defendant**), you need to know the strengths and weaknesses of the other side's case in order to make your own best case. The more you read about both sides, the better prepared you will be.

The material in this book is organized to make it easy for you to get "the big picture" first with general information about small claims courts and what those courts can and cannot do. Next is information about how to handle typical types of cases, with specific information for plaintiffs and for defendants. Finally, you can look at ways to collect money owed to you after you win your case.

You may be tempted to skim the table of contents for a particular topic of interest and read only that part of this book. Remember, though, that you will not be the only person in the courtroom. The person on the other side of the case will do things and say things to persuade the judge to rule the other way. The judge may be unfamiliar with the particular law that you think supports your position, and you will need to know how to educate the judge about that law and how you think it applies to you.

Unfortunately, even small claims court, where lawyers don't appear, suffers from the use of "legalese." So, when a law-related term appears for the first time here, it will be in **bold-face type**. If you're not sure of its meaning, you can turn to the glossary at the end of the book for a definition or description of the term.

You'll find other resources at the end of the book, too. In Appendix A, you will see the **Oregon Revised Statutes (ORS)** and **Uniform Trial Court Rules (UTCR)** that apply to small claims court generally.

xiv

WARNING: The courts and the legislature change the law and the rules from time to time. The information in this book is accurate as of July 2019, but you should always check to make sure the law still applies later on.

Appendix B directs you to helpful information about topics that are often the subject of disputes in small claims court. This appendix also refers you to lawyers who may be able to provide free or low-cost legal advice or representation in your case.

All of Oregon's counties do things a little differently from each other. The court clerks' hours may be different; the forms you must file to start or respond to a case may be different. The cost to file a case may be different. In some counties, small claims may be decided by a full-time judge while in others a local lawyer may sometimes fill in as a temporary judge (a **pro tem**). Some counties offer a chance to **mediate** your case. Appendix C tells you how to contact your court for further information for your own case.

CHAPTER 1

Small claims court: Is it for you?

There are plenty of reasons to choose—and not to choose—small claims court. They include the amount of money (if any) that's at stake, what you want a court to do about your problem, whether you can afford a lawyer, and whether the case is too complicated for you to do on your own. There are other considerations, too, that will be discussed later. Knowing what small claims court is and does is the first step in making the decision.

What is a small claims court?

Small claims court was created to give people a quick, inexpensive way to solve some kinds of legal problems, without having to resort to the help of an attorney in the courtroom. Every state's small claims system is a little different.

Most people who use small claims court in Oregon represent themselves. (Lawyers are usually not allowed to appear in small claim courts; neither, generally, is a friend or other "representative.") Trials in small claims cases are scheduled much faster than trials in regular (**circuit**) court cases. The strict rules of evidence used in circuit court do not apply in small claims court; compared to circuit court trials, small claims hearings are relatively informal and usually quite short. There are small claims courts throughout the state. See Appendix C for a full listing, with contact information.

What is a "small claim" in Oregon?

Oregon's small claims courts handle cases in which the plaintiff claims to be entitled to no more than $10,000 in money or property from the defendant. That $10,000 can take several forms. Oregon law says small claims court can be used for the "recovery of money, damages, specific personal property, or any penalty or forfeiture." ORS 46.405(2).

- If someone owes you money, you can sue in small claims court to get your money back.
- If someone has damaged or destroyed your property or caused you an injury, you can sue for **damages**—the value of the harm done. In some cases, you can sue—or be sued—for statutory damages. **Statutory damages** are a set amount or a range of amounts of money that the law says is owed for certain kinds of improper conduct. This amount can be higher than the amount of actual financial loss the plaintiff has suffered. Sometimes a written contract that is in dispute will call for **liquidated damages**—an amount that the parties agreed, when entering into the contract, would be a reasonable amount to cover the financial harm a breach of the contract might cause. In a very few cases, a plaintiff may be entitled to **punitive damages**—similar to a fine imposed on a **party** that has deliberately or recklessly caused harm to you and does not seem willing to stop its bad conduct.
- You can use small claims court to get back belongings that someone has wrongfully taken or wrongfully refuses to give back, so long as the value you claim is $10,000 or less. For example, you sold a dog to someone who didn't make all the payments for it. You can ask the court to order the buyer to give the dog back or pay you the rest of what is owed. **Exception: Small claims court is *not* where you ask for your belongings back if they have been taken by the landlord at your current or former home. There is a very fast circuit court process you must use for this purpose. The circuit court clerk's office has special forms for getting back belongings taken by residential landlords.**
- Small claims court allows people to file claims for **penalties** and **forfeitures**, too. Typically, a penalty is a remedy that governments use—such as daily fines for a continuing violation of a local ordinance. In some places, a municipal hearing officer handles these cases. A contract may allow for a forfeiture of an item if a purchaser violates the contract—but only if the court agrees that the purchaser has breached the contract.

Some examples can help explain what these categories mean.

Recovery of money:

Justin lent his cousin $800 six months ago. According to a written promise the cousin signed, the cousin was to pay back the money two months ago. Now the cousin won't pay. Justin can sue for recovery of the money he lent.

Recovery of specific personal property:

Brittany is filing a small claims case against her former "best friend" after the friend came uninvited to Brittany's apartment and "borrowed" her laptop and printer without her permission. The police refused to intervene. The equipment is worth $950. Brittany will sue for the return of her belongings, or, in the alternative, the cost of the equipment. A case that is filed to get back belongings is sometimes called a case in **replevin.**

Damages:

1. Ellen is suing for the value of a new cashmere sweater after she took it for its first cleaning to her neighborhood dry cleaner—and the sweater came back two sizes too small. Ellen's case is for **actual damages,** the full cost of her nearly new sweater, with her claim based on the dry cleaner's negligent treatment of her sweater. (If the sweater were not new, her actual damages would be lower.)

2. Ricardo sues an auto repair shop for an unlawful trade practice after a "new" battery he bought for $70 turned out to be a used battery that died of old age a week after he bought it. Ricardo could sue for actual damages, but he will sue instead for statutory damages based on a state law that provides a damages award of $200 based on the unlawful practice.

3. After a landlord rents out a house in a residential neighborhood to obvious drug dealers, the next-door neighbors sue the landlord for damages caused by this "private nuisance"—the noise and traffic caused by the constant comings and goings of drug purchasers, the needles and other discarded drug paraphernalia that shows up on their lawns, etc. The neighbors' cases will seek actual damages, caused by the decrease in their privacy and enjoyment of their property. (For more information about this type of situation, see Chapter 9.)

4. Erin, the owner of a small jewelry store, files a case against a customer who paid for a $200 amethyst ring with a bad check. Because Erin gave the customer a written notice to make payment more than 30 days ago and there was no payment, she is entitled to a judgment for statutory damages of $600—three times the price of the ring, plus interest, and her costs connected with the bank's dishonoring the check.

5. Cliff, a residential landlord, will sue a former tenant for one month's rent after the tenant moved out without giving Cliff 30 days' written notice that she was leaving. The tenant had promised under the rental agreement to give notice or be held liable for the rent for that period. Despite his best efforts, Cliff was unable to rent the unit right away, so he is entitled to the amount of rent that was lost for up to one month's value.

Cases that can't go to small claims court

Not every case can go to small claims court, even if the amount of the claim is $10,000 or less. You cannot file a **class action** lawsuit (where a few plaintiffs stand up on behalf of many more people with claims they have in common) in small claims court. Nor, with only one narrow exception, can you get a small claims court to give you an **injunction**—a court order that forces the other party to stop unlawful conduct against you. If you are in jail or prison, even if you have not yet had a trial, you may not file a claim against another prisoner in small claims court.

Other limits on your rights in small claims court

You do not have the right to a jury trial in a small claims case, nor the right to appeal from a small claims court decision--except when your small claims case starts out in **justice court** rather than in the small claims department of a circuit court. Even there, you can appeal only to the circuit court for a new trial, and only in limited circumstances.

Who is a "party" in a small claims case?

A **party** is someone who either starts a court case as a plaintiff or must respond to the case as a defendant. There can be more than one party on each side. The party can be an individual or a small business, a for-profit or non-profit organization, or even a political entity like a state agency or department, a city or county, or a government district—a school district, an irrigation district, etc.

A party can be someone who took over the rights of someone else—for example, a debt collection agency that has taken over the claim of an original creditor for payment of money owed to that creditor. A party can be a child, whom an adult (usually a parent) represents. Even someone who is no longer alive can be a party (his or her interests are handled by the administrator of the dead person's estate).

If you are a potential plaintiff, it will be important to name the right people as defendants. If you win your case, your victory will be meaningless if you cannot enforce it against the people who were actually responsible for your problem. As you read further, you'll get some tips on finding and naming the right defendant. And there are special considerations to take into account when you file a case against businesses and governmental entities, considerations that will be discussed in Chapter 2.

If you are a defendant or potential defendant, you may not recognize the name of the person or company suing you. There are several possible reasons for this situation:

- The original claimant may have given or sold (**assigned**) its rights against you to someone else. Assignment is what allows collection agencies to sue for a debt owed to a business, for example.

- You may be sued in a few instances for the unlawful conduct of someone else—such as when parents are sued for intentional bad acts of their minor children.
- You may be sued for someone else's debt if you co-signed a loan with that person and the person didn't repay the loan.
- The plaintiff may be going after the wrong person!

As a defendant, you'll learn what to do when you know the plaintiff is naming you by mistake. This problem has become much more common in recent years because of the growth in the crime of identity theft and the rise of big "debt buyer" collection agencies that may not verify information carefully.

Is it better to have an attorney?

Deciding whether to represent yourself in small claims court or to hire an attorney to represent you in circuit court is one of the harder decisions you may have to make in your case. Lawyers are expensive. But having a lawyer can offer you significant advantages: the law can be very complicated. A capable lawyer can help you identify and develop claims you may not know you have. If you are a defendant, a lawyer can help with defenses against those claims.

Among the factors you should weigh when making this decision are these:

1. If your claim is for $750 or less and the case type is one that does not entitle you to **statutory attorney fees** if you win the case, your claim must be filed in small claims court. (Some kinds of consumer cases, landlord-tenant matters, bounced-check cases, and others are based on statutes that commonly allow for attorney fees even when the damages you claim are small. In those kinds of cases, you can choose to file in circuit court if you have an attorney, rather than filing in small claims court.)
2. If your claim is between $751 and $10,000, you can choose to have your case heard in circuit court, where you may be represented by an attorney. In most of these cases, you will participate in pre-trial arbitration. There is an additional cost for this process.
3. If your claim is for more than $10,000, your case must go to circuit court, whether you have a lawyer or not. Arbitration is usually necessary.
4. A case filed in circuit court normally takes many months to come to trial. A case filed in small claims court goes to trial within about six weeks to three months of filing, although once in a while the wait may

be a little longer.

5. Most cases filed in circuit court end without a trial because the attorneys in the case negotiate a solution or an arbitrator makes a decision that the parties decide they can live with. A larger percentage of cases in small claims court go all the way to hearing, especially in counties where the courts do not offer a mediation program for small claims cases.

6. If you have no money for a lawyer and a lawyer will not represent you without charging you, you have no choice. You must represent yourself.

7. If a case is complex (such as a medical or legal malpractice claim, a claim about a dangerous or defective product, or a case in which only the other side has all or most of the proof about what happened), having a lawyer can make a big difference. Lawyers know how to force the other party to turn over information you need so you can prove your case. Lawyers know how to get information from expert witnesses likely to be involved in the case.

8. The cost of a lawyer may be worth it to get a good result. On the other hand, nothing guarantees a good result.

9. Filing and going through a lawsuit is stressful. Even if you win your case, you will likely feel "beaten up" by the time it's all over. Having a lawyer can sometimes make the process feel less stressful.

10. If you have the option of filing your case in circuit court, that forum comes with the right to appeal if the judge misapplies the law to your case. There is no right to appeal from small claims court unless the case started in justice court.

If you want to hire an attorney but don't have the money to do so, you may be able to get free or low-cost help through a law school legal clinic or a legal aid program. There's a big demand for these services, though, so don't count on these resources unless and until one of them agrees to help you. Sometimes these programs know about lawyers in private practice who will take a case like yours **pro bono**—without charging you. See Appendix B for more information about these resources.

Some kinds of cases—consumer claims and landlords and tenants' rights claims—may be based on laws that require the party that loses the case to pay the attorney fees of the party that wins the case. Or, if your case involves a written contract, the contract may say that one party or the **prevailing party** is entitled to attorney fees from the other side. A lawyer in private practice may be willing to help you if your case is strong and one of these attorney-fee rights exists.

Generally, the law does not provide for the losing side to pay the winner's attorney fees in cases involving **torts** (harm done to a person or property either negligently or intentionally) or **contract** (unless the language of a written contract says otherwise). Still, there are a couple of laws that may be helpful to you in convincing a private lawyer to take this kind of case. They allow for the lawyer to get attorney fees from the other side if you win.

Here's an example of one of those laws:

A state statute, ORS 20.080, applies to damages claims of up to $10,000 for harm done to a person or property (tort cases). Four things determine whether the lawyer can get fees from the other side. First, the plaintiff or the plaintiff's lawyer must send a letter to the defendant asking for payment of the plaintiff's claim (a **demand letter**) at least 30 days before you file your claim. (If you have already filed the small claims case, and the defendant asks for a jury trial, then the demand letter must be sent up to 30 days after the case has been transferred to circuit court, where the parties can have a jury.) Second, if you refuse an offer of money from the defendant to settle the case before trial and the judge rules at trial that you aren't entitled to any more than the defendant offered, your lawyer is awarded no fee. Third, if the defendant raises his or her own claim against you (a **counterclaim**) in the same case and wins the case, your lawyer would get no attorney fee award—and that person's lawyer could win attorney fees against you. Fourth, even if you win hands down, the defendant may have no money to pay your lawyer's fee, even if the court awards it. The lawyer will likely then turn to you for payment, unless you agreed otherwise at the beginning of the case.

A similar statute, ORS 20.082, covers most contracts and documented debts (that is, debts that are put in writing) of up to $10,000. The same traps described above apply here. Seeing how these laws play out, you can understand why some attorneys cannot be convinced to take on one of these cases without at least some payment from you in advance. Still, you may be able to get representation if your case is strong and your claim is for a reasonable amount.

Even if you can't get full representation when you want it, you likely can get low-cost or free legal advice about your case. In fact, quite a few people who go it alone have gotten legal advice about their rights before they march into the courtroom. Getting that reality check from someone knowledgeable and objective can help you determine how and even whether to go forward with a small claims case. For some sources of free and low-cost advice and information, see Appendix B at the end of this book.

Is the problem worth all the trouble of going to court?

If only there were a simple answer to this question! The three things you need to consider in order to answer this question are:

- How likely am I to win this case?
- What if I win, but the defendant has no money for me to collect after I've gotten a **judgment** against him or her?
- Can I handle the anxiety and stress involved in a lawsuit?

The first question is the one the judge in your case ultimately has to wrestle with: does your case "have merit"? That is, does the law support your position? Doing your homework before filing a case is really important, because if the law is against your position, you are almost certainly going to lose the argument, the case, and some money for court costs and filing fees—and potentially owe the defendant money for a **counterclaim** he or she might file.

Before starting your case, do some reading about your rights; look at helpful internet sites about the law that applies; ask sensible friends if they think you are being reasonable; and, if at all possible, talk to an attorney about whether you are likely to win your case. Sometimes, there is no law to protect people from certain kinds of harms. Or even though you've been hurt by someone else's behavior, you don't have the evidence you need to back up your position. In situations like these, it may be best to walk away, sadder but wiser.

On the other hand, there are times when it's not a good idea to walk away. Over the years, many, many clients have told me about truly terrible injustices that they endured years ago but did nothing about—and those wrongs have been eating at them ever since. By the time they finally talk to a lawyer, it's much too late for them to do anything. So if knowledgeable people tell you that you have a strong case, think twice before giving up without a fight. You don't want to be regretful later on.

To answer the second question, make a realistic assessment of how likely you are to get what you are asking for if you win your case. The court decision in your favor simply gives you the right to use certain methods to collect what you are owed—small claims court will not collect the money for you. **In some cases, collecting can be difficult or impossible.** For example, if you are hoping to get payment from someone whose only income is government disability benefits, you likely will not be able to collect any money from that person no matter how successful you are in the courtroom. Likewise, you may be wasting your time going after someone who is going to board the bus in the next few days for a long haul in federal prison. If there is a way for you to get even part of your money without filing a court case in these and similar situations, give the idea serious consideration. See Chapter 11 for more details about "exempt" income and resources. Chapter 11 also contains information on methods of collecting what you are owed—or owe.

For the third question, ask yourself whether you can take on the commitment to handle your case effectively, and put up with the stress and uncertainty that is a part of preparing every court case. Preparing well for court often takes time. Researching the law, finding and interviewing witnesses, tracking down documents, practicing the presentation you will make to the court, and watching other court proceedings so you understand the do's and dont's of the courtroom can require patience and stamina. If preparation requires travel or taking time off from work, you cannot include those costs as part of your claim.

Alternatives to court
Community mediation

For a few kinds of cases, free or low-cost community mediation programs may be available to you. Through these services, professionals and trained volunteers invite disputing community members to meet together in an attempt to work out their differences. This kind of service won't help you negotiate with a collection agency, but it may be able to get your cousin to understand why it's important to you to get back the money you lent him six months ago, or to convince your next-door neighbor that 6 a.m. is a bad time to use his power mower.

Mediation helps people come up with their own solutions to problems, rather than letting a busy judge make a decision for them. The service is often free. The community mediation process is purely voluntary; the other side doesn't have to agree to participate, but many people do agree. Most people who try mediation are very satisfied with the outcome.

If you try a community mediation program and mediation either doesn't work for you or the other party doesn't follow through with the agreement you worked out together, you can still take your claim to court. It's important to remember, however, that the time limit for filing your claim (the **statute of limitations**) doesn't stop while you try to work out your problem through mediation.

To find out if your community has mediation services, see the Oregon Community Mediation Programs website, http://www.ormediation.org/, or contact the city or the county for information. Law enforcement agencies often know about local programs like this, too. If there is a community mediation program, find out whether it can handle your problem.

Court-sponsored mediation

Some small claims courts offer (or require) a consultation with a court mediator after a case has been filed and before it goes to trial. The trained mediator works with the parties to try to find an acceptable solution. If the parties come to agreement, they then report that agreement to the judge when they have their hearing or submit their signed agreement. In most cases, the judge accepts the agreement (known as a **stipulated dismissal**) and dismisses the case contingent on the parties' following through with their agreement— preventing a **judgment** against one of the parties that could hurt his or her credit record.

The parties do not have to come to an agreement. Furthermore, any discussion during mediation cannot be brought up in court. That conversation is confidential.

"But it's the principle of the thing!"

We have all heard the stories of courageous people who demanded justice through the courts. None of these cases started in small claims court. Small claims court is not the place to go if your mission is to change the world.

Think hard about what your goal is in filing your case. If your only argument is "It's the principle of the thing," or if you are looking solely for vengeance, you are very unlikely to be satisfied with the result you get in court. If you think that the law that applies to your case is unfair, your voice needs to be heard by legislators—the people who made the law—not by judges, who have a duty to apply the law as it exists even if they disagree with it.

What if you're the one being sued?

As a defendant, you have to make some of the same decisions that the plaintiff in your case had to make—only a lot faster. In Oregon, you have only 14 days from the time you receive your court papers in which to file an **answer** (in small claims court it's called a **defendant's election**) or a counterclaim, or both. Just like potential plaintiffs, defendants are wise to get some legal advice if they possibly can before deciding whether to fight the claim in court. See Appendix B for some free or low-cost resources. For some guidance on how to evaluate your chances in various kinds of cases, see Chapters 7, 8, and 9.

CHAPTER 2

Overview of the small claims process

The simplest part of any small claims case is the procedure for getting into court. First, the plaintiff figures out where to file the case (see the last section in this chapter), and files it. Then, the defendant gets formal notice of the claim from the plaintiff (see Chapter 3), and decides whether to fight the case. If the defendant files nothing, the plaintiff wins the case and gets a judgment by **default**. If the defendant files defenses or counterclaims within the small claims dollar limit, the case is set for a trial (some courts call it a "hearing").

A judge makes a ruling (often at the time of the trial, but sometimes later on) that one side or the other wins the case. If the losing party ends up owing money to the winning side and doesn't pay, the winner can then take steps to collect the debt, interest on the debt, costs of filing and **service of process**, and a prevailing party fee.

Plaintiffs: before you file

Although the process of getting the cases into court is predictable and straightforward, every case is based on different facts. And there is always some preparation you must do before you file. These things are what you, as a plaintiff, must do before filing your case:

1. Place a money value on your case;
2. Determine that the property you want back or the money you plan to sue for will fit within the small claims court limit of $10,000, or decide

you are willing to ask for less than the value in order to use small claims court;

3. Do enough research about the law to conclude that your claim is justified;
4. Figure out who and where the correct defendants are, and what kind of notice they are entitled to;
5. Attempt to settle the dispute without success, including by mediation (see Chapter 1); and
6. Decide which small claims court you would need to use.

Valuing your case for small claims court

Even though the limit for small claims court is $10,000, you can ask only for the amount that is lawfully due to you. The court, in turn, may give you what you ask for or less, depending on the facts of the case. That possibility makes it very important for you to be able to justify to the court why you picked the amount you did. Sometimes putting a dollar value on your case is easy.

Here are a couple of examples:

If your so-called friend "borrowed" your new computer, you will ask the court for the return of that computer in good condition or for the value of the computer. If the computer has been in use for a while, you are unlikely to be able to claim its full cost (its "replacement" value). You may have to take extra steps to prove your claim is worth what you say it is—statements from computer dealers about current value, ads in newspapers or on www.craigslist. com showing comparable values of used equipment, etc.

You also want to consider the full scope of your loss. For example, if you bought a "new" battery from a dishonest mechanic and the battery, actually quite old, failed a week later while you were on your way to work, you might sue simply for your money back. But perhaps you had to pay for a tow truck or you paid a friend to rescue you and take you to work; you may have lost wages for the two hours you were delayed at your job; and, of course, you had to buy another battery. Any of these expenses would be a natural consequence of your reliance on the "new" battery. In addition, consumer protection laws may entitle you to statutory damages that are higher than the actual expenses you incurred if your damages are the result of false statements. See Chapter 8 for more information about consumer protection laws.

Sometimes putting a dollar value on your case is more complex. Think about whether you're eligible for **statutory damages** instead of or in addition to your actual loss before you put a dollar amount on your claim. (Oregon's landlord-tenant laws and federal and state consumer laws typically provide for statutory damages.) Also think about whether you have more than one claim against the defendant.

Here are a couple of examples:

A reckless driver knocked down your mailbox stand and then ran over your prize peonies and your Russian wolfhound before regaining control of his car. Oregon law treats these three things as one claim because they all came about from a single incident involving the same defendant. If the loss exceeds $10,000, you cannot separate the claims into more than one case. Instead, you must either file your case in circuit court or, if you remain in small claims court, limit the amount for which you are suing to $10,000 even though your losses were higher. If you win, you cannot file another case for the balance of your losses from the same incident. You got all you're going to get. Likewise, if you lose the case, you cannot re-file the whole case or any part of the case later on.

If you want the defendant to pay back money you lent her last year and you also want her to pay for the bicycle she backed over in your driveway this year, you have two claims. If they are worth less than $10,000 together, you can raise both claims in one case because they each involve the same defendant. You also can raise these claims as two separate cases because they did not involve the same incident, although you would have to pay a separate filing fee for each case.

Researching the law

A number of resources can help you research what your rights—and the defendant's rights—are. Some Oregon counties have law libraries, with helpful and knowledgeable staff, open to the public. Staff are not lawyers and can't give legal advice, but they can often point you in the right direction. Some county law libraries are not maintained or staffed; they may have outdated or incomplete information that is not very helpful.

Almost all law libraries and many public libraries—including those at universities and community colleges--have state laws (Oregon Revised Statutes, or ORS), however. The ORS is available online, too, free at www.leg.state.or.us/ors. Other free online resources include www.findlaw.com, www.law.cornell.edu, and www.nolo.com. Extremely helpful for some kinds of consumer cases is www.nclc.org, the website of the National Consumer Law Center. In addition, consumers can learn about some of their rights under state law at the Oregon Attorney General's website, www.doj.state.or.us. General information about specific legal topics, including consumer and landlord-tenant law, is available free at www.oregonlawhelp.org and for the public page of the Oregon State Bar website, www.osbar.org. See Appendix B for more resources.

The Oregon State Bar publishes a large assortment of manuals, primarily for use by lawyers, that can be very helpful. (Unfortunately, they are written in dense legalese, so they can sometimes also be pretty confusing.) These books cover such topics as real estate disputes, consumer rights, debtor and creditor rights, arbitration and mediation, torts and contracts, employment rights, and trial practice. Look at Appendix B for a partial list of these manuals. Law libraries sometimes have these volumes, along with legal training materials on many topics, on their shelves; they generally have them available online, too.

Who's the real defendant?

The **real party in interest** should always be the person or entity you name as the defendant. And sometimes the real party in interest in your case won't be obvious.

Here's an example:

You realize you have to sue your former landlord for failing to return your security deposit after you moved out. You know the address of your apartment building and you know the nickname of the resident manager—"Madge." To file your case, though, you need to know the name of the owner, because that's the person who has your money and is responsible for returning the deposit. In other words, the owner is the **real party in interest** in your case. If Madge won't tell you the name and address of the owner and if the owner's name and contact information are not on your rental agreement, you can usually find out from the county tax assessor, in the county where the apartment building is, based on where the property tax bill goes. Once you have this information, you should double-check with the county recorder's office in the county where the property is to verify that the taxpayer is also the owner of the property. Sometimes a local title company will give you the information, too. If the property is in the names of more than one individual, you will want to name all of them as defendants— if you can locate them all. Note: You also have the right under Oregon landlord-tenant law to name Madge as a defendant if the landlord didn't identify itself in your rental agreement.

It's not always clear who is the real party in interest. Here are a couple of examples that illustrate the problem.

A salesperson at a local Ford dealership lied to you about the condition of a used car, and you relied on the salesperson's assurances--ending up with The Car From Hell. Suing later over this unfair trade practice, you may wonder whether to name as the defendant the salesperson, the dealership, or the Ford Motor Company—or all three of them. It's very unlikely that Ford Motor Company has any involvement with the problem. In such a case, you would probably name only the salesperson and perhaps the dealership. (See "Finding the defendant—a business or corporation," below.)

You pull up to the drive-up window at your favorite burger place. The worker who takes your order is goofing around, and tries to execute a fancy pass with your order—drenching your new suede jacket with soda pop. He refuses to pay for the damage. The manager says the damage is the employee's fault, so the restaurant will not pay, either. The jacket cost you $375, and your dry cleaner says it's ruined. Who should get sued? As a general rule, an employee who causes harm or damage when the employee is acting "within the scope of his or her duties" will not be liable to you—the business where the employee works will be liable. If the worker was doing what he was being paid to do—greet customers, take orders, and serve food—it's likely his employer will be liable for his negligence even if the employee was goofing around (but sometimes it is hard to tell for sure). If you are in doubt about who might be legally responsible, get some legal advice. If the answer is still unclear, sue both the individual and the employer.

Finding the defendant—an individual

In the cases described earlier in this chapter, you won't have any trouble figuring out who the defendant is. It's important to put the defendant's full legal name—including middle names or initials and "junior," "senior," etc.—on the court papers, however. No nicknames! If you think the defendant might go by more than one name, list on your court papers all names you know of, like this:

> Bubba Jones, aka ("also known as") Walter Z. Jones, aka
> Tobias Martin Johnson

When you have trouble finding the defendant

Finding individuals is easier than it used to be, thanks to the Internet. Still, some people can be difficult to track. A visit to Google, www.peoplesearch. com, www.zabasearch.com, or www.spokeo.com should net you at least some of the information you need. Some public libraries still collect telephone directories, where you can sometimes find a person with a listed phone. You may have difficulty if a defendant has a common name, however.

Another relatively easy way to find a person in order to serve court papers is to get the addresses from Driver and Motor Vehicle Services (DMV)—if the person is licensed to drive in Oregon. After you have filed your case, the person you select to serve the papers can file a "Request for Information" at DMV. The form you need, Form 735-7122, is available online and at any DMV field office. The person who will try to serve the papers must identify himself or herself on the form as a process server, and send in the request with the required fee. For more information about obtaining information from DMV, call (503) 945-5475 weekdays or log onto www.odot.state.or.us/dmv/. Other states' DMV websites should offer similar guidance for obtaining addresses.

Sometimes it is possible to find someone through the post office, using a Freedom of Information Act (FOIA) request form. All post office branches have this form. You must justify your request for the search and pay a small charge. The post office decides whether you have a good enough reason to get access to the information. Even if the post office is able to help you, the search may take time—from days to several weeks.

Defendants in special situations

Naming the right defendant becomes more complicated when the case is against:

- A minor;
- A person who is legally mentally incompetent (lacks **capacity**); or
- A person who has died.

When the defendant is a minor

Special rules apply when the potential defendant is a minor. When the minor is younger than 14, you must **serve** the claim and notice on the minor and on a parent or guardian, or, if there is no parent or guardian, the person responsible for taking care of the minor, the minor's employer in a case related to the minor's job, or a **guardian ad litem** (someone appointed by the court to represent the minor's interests). You may be the one who has to ask the court (by formal **motion**) to appoint someone to act as the guardian ad litem; if so, you will probably need the help of a lawyer to do that. Oregon court rules don't require notice to a responsible adult when the minor is 14 or older. See ORCP 7 D (3) and ORCP 27A. This special service isn't needed in cases arising under the Oregon Residential Landlord and Tenant Act. Nor is it necessary if the minor is married or legally emancipated by a court.

There are a couple of other twists related to suits against minors. The law says that minors lack the "legal capacity" to sue or be sued. In other words, according to the law they don't understand enough about their rights or the legal consequences of their actions so as to make informed decisions. The law says further that because they lack capacity, they cannot be bound to any contract they enter into—except for the basic necessities (shelter, food, medical care). If you sold an iPod to a 15-year-old on credit, you will be wasting your time suing for payment.

Minors are held responsible for torts they commit (intentional or reckless behavior). Under Oregon law, the intentional torts minors commit (vandalism, thefts, arson, etc.) result in limited liability for their custodial parent or guardian—up to $7,500. In such cases, ORS 30.765 requires service not only on the minor but also on the parent or guardian, regardless of the age of the minor.

When the defendant is mentally incompetent or has died

If a court has decided that the defendant is mentally incompetent, you would serve the person's legal **guardian** or a **conservator**. Because a court decides who a guardian or conservator will be, that person's name will be in court records.

If the defendant is no longer living, you will have to serve the personal representative of the person's estate. If no one is named as personal representative within 60 days of the person's death, you will need to ask the court to appoint one. The process can be complicated; in these situations, it is advisable to get help from a lawyer. Court clerks in the probate department of circuit court can provide helpful information, too—but not legal advice.

When the defendant is on active military duty

Special rules apply when a defendant is on active duty in the National Guard or the military and thus is unable to participate in a court hearing. While you can file your case and serve the defendant, you normally cannot get a default judgment against a service member who isn't free to appear in court to defend himself or herself. State law provides for significant damages against a plaintiff who ignores a written request from a service member asking for a delay in the case or who files for a default judgment knowing the service member is on active military duty. The service member may have additional remedies against you under the federal Service Members' Civil Relief Act.

If you know the defendant's first and last names and date of birth or Social Security number, you may be able to find out definitively from the federal government whether the defendant is currently on active duty. The Department of Defense has active-duty status information at www.dmdc.osd.mil/appj/scra/scraHome.do.

When the defendant has filed for bankruptcy

In bankruptcy cases, the bankruptcy court always orders a temporary **stay** in all other cases against the party who filed for bankruptcy. You can be held in contempt of court for trying to advance your case during the stay.

Finding the defendant—a business or corporation

If you plan to sue a business, you may find out that the owner is not an individual but an entity, such as Landlords, Inc., or Landlords LLP, or Landlords LLC, or Randy Land and Sandy Lord DBA Landlords. A corporation name or a business name that is anything other than the name of the owner is called an **assumed business name**. If that's the kind of name you are looking at, you will need to do a little more research to determine whom to name as defendants in your case, how to list their names as defendants on your court papers, and also how to serve court papers on these defendants. For that matter, if you are filing a small claims case *on behalf of* a business, you must follow the same rules as the ones that apply to defendants when you are naming your own business on the court papers. The rules are below.

1. **A business that belongs to a single individual as a "sole proprietorship"** will be named like this:

   Randy Land DBA (doing business as) Landlords
   physical address and mailing address, if different

2. **A business that belongs to more than one individual as a partnership will be named like this:**

   Randy Land and Sandy Lord DBA Landlords,
   a partnership (physical address and mailing address of each)

3. **A corporation** will be named like this:

Landlords, Inc.	**Serve** registered agent: Albert Vermin
12 Twelfth Street	212 N. Fourth
Portland OR 97204	Portland OR 97205

4. **A corporation with an assumed business name ("doing business as" or "DBA")** will be named like this:

Landlords, Inc.	**Serve** registered agent: Albert Vermin
DBA Luxury Apartments	212 N. Fourth
12 Twelfth Street	Portland OR 97205
Portland OR 97204	

There are a couple of ways to find out who and where these defendants are. You can call the Corporations Division of the Oregon Secretary of State in

Salem at (503) 986-2200 (weekdays 8 a.m. to 4:45 p.m.) or look online at sos. oregon.gov/business/pages/find.aspx to see the names of businesses registered in Oregon. Many cities and counties require businesses to obtain local licenses; they too should have names and addresses of proprietors and partners.

As you can see from these examples, business entities are required to have a registered agent. The agent, not the business, gets served the court papers, even though the business itself is named as the defendant. If a business with an assumed name or a corporation is not registered, and you cannot find out its legal status or its address, you have the right to serve the court papers on the business by sending the papers directly to the business in care of the Secretary of State's office. Note: A business that is **not** incorporated or that does not have an assumed business name does not have to register with the Secretary of State (example: John Cochran, attorney at law); in that situation, you simply sue the individual or individuals.

When the defendant can't be found

Can your case go forward if you can't find the defendant? Yes, although you will have to go through several extra steps. Some of those extra steps are outlined above—looking in phone books, checking with DMV or the secretary of state, using online resources, asking friends and neighbors of the prospective defendant where the person might be, etc. If you do contact family and acquaintances, do not tell them why you are searching for the defendant. Why? In some situations, claiming that someone owes you money can result in a claim against you for unlawful debt collection. It's important to keep records of all the steps you take to find the defendant because you will need that information later on to show a judge that you have made every reasonable effort to find the defendant.

If every reasonable effort to find the defendant is unsuccessful, Oregon law allows **service** on a prospective defendant by publishing notice of the case in a general newspaper, by posting notice of the case in public places, and other ways that might actually alert someone that he or she is being sued. The plaintiff must first get permission from the court in order to use these other methods, however, and will have to demonstrate that he or she did make a significant effort to locate the defendant. (By the time you read this, the State of Oregon or the state where the defendant lives may have an official "Legal Notices" website that would suit this purpose.)

If these methods are unsuccessful, too, the lawsuit can still go forward. You have made your best effort to give the defendant notice even if you could not find him or her. If the defendant does not file an answer in the case, you win the case by **default**. Once you win it, though, you may have a very difficult time getting payment from someone you can't find. In short, when you can't locate the defendant, you are faced with deciding whether to sue now and perhaps be unable to collect, or to wait until you can find the defendant before suing—and possibly letting the time limit for a lawsuit go by while you wait, so that it is then too late to file a case.

Attempting to settle the case

Before a plaintiff can file a case in small claims court, the plaintiff must make a reasonable effort to settle the matter. The small claims court rule to try to settle claims before filing a court case comes from the wisdom that people who try to work things out usually can.

The plaintiff has to state under oath on the complaint that he or she has tried to solve the problem before using the courts; being untruthful under oath can certainly be held against you when the judge is deciding whose side of the story to believe. Just as important as making the attempt to settle, the plaintiff must be prepared to demonstrate to a judge that he or she made the attempt. The law doesn't require you to put your efforts in writing, but doing so is often a very good idea. (If you don't do so, a defendant may claim to the judge that the filing of the case was the first time she'd heard anything about the problem—and you may have no proof to the contrary. The result could be that the judge throws out your case. And you won't get a refund of your filing fee.)

One way to show this effort is with a copy of a letter sent to the defendant for that purpose. Your letter can:

- Propose a solution, with a reasonable deadline for the defendant to respond. Then you must wait for the deadline to pass.
- Document other efforts to settle, for example, "This letter confirms that I called you last week to discuss when you will pay me for the fence I built for you. At that time, you told me nothing doing, and said you'd see me in court."

All letters proposing or confirming a settlement should be dated. They should, to the extent possible, state the dates on which you and the defendant discussed the problem in the past, and, if necessary, describe the problem. Obviously, you need to make and keep a copy of the letter. Some lawyers recommend that you send such a letter by both regular and certified mail with a return receipt. (If the defendant accepts the certified letter, you have proof it was received. If the letter you sent by regular mail was properly addressed, had sufficient postage, and listed your return address, the law presumes the defendant received it.) See examples of settlement letters at the end of this chapter.

It is important that any letter you write be accurate and respectful. If you must use the letter in court later on and the letter is rude or exaggerates your claim, you—not the defendant—will look bad as a result.

If you wrote a letter but didn't keep a copy, tell the judge when you sent the letter, how you sent it, and whether it came back to you marked "undeliverable." If it didn't come back, the law presumes that the defendant got it. If you haven't written a letter, it is important to document what you have done—telephone calls (how many and when, what result); conversations in person (how many and when, what result). If you have phone records of your calls to the defendant, those can help support your claim. Someone may have witnessed your side of the phone call or your in-person conversations with the defendant; the witness can be helpful to your case.

Don't be surprised when the judge doesn't want to know what you offered or what the defendant proposed to settle your case. The judge needs to know only that you made a good-faith effort and were unable to resolve the problem before you filed your case.

Defendants entitled to special notice

Government entities are entitled to specific formal notice about one type of claim—one alleging a **tort**--*before* you file your claim and within a certain period of time after you suffer harm as a result of the defendant's action or failure to act. Many plaintiffs are unaware of this requirement, and lose their chance to make their case as a result.

Some examples:

- Tribally owned casinos and tribal governments: the basis for liability and the procedure and time limit for notice of a tort claim will be found in the tribal code, which often is not available at county law libraries. Each tribe has its own procedures. You may find that you must file a case in tribal court, if it is the only court with legal jurisdiction.
- State and local governments, including irrigation, transportation, and school districts; public universities and colleges; and regional governments

In most cases against state or local governments, you have no more than 180 days after the problem arises in which to make a written claim for compensation for the harm. ORS 30.275 describes the time limits more fully. It also specifies the information your claim must contain, and the official to whom you must send the claim notice. You must keep a copy of the claim notice to show the court if you then must file a lawsuit.

There are many limitations on tort cases against state and local governments, making filing in small claims court quite difficult. Most of the limitations are listed in ORS 30.260 to ORS 30.268. For example, a government or agency is not liable for bad conduct of an employee who is not performing his or her duties or following the law—unless the agency knows of the bad conduct and allows it. In a tort claim case, it is extremely important to review the facts of your situation with an attorney before you take any action. Sometimes you may not have a claim against the agency but may still have a claim against the employee. When the answer isn't clear, consider naming both the individual and the agency.

Jail or prison inmates (including people who are waiting for their trials) face additional hurdles in these cases. See Chapter 9 for more information.

Bars, taverns, people who serve alcoholic drinks at their homes, and ski resorts also are entitled to get written notice of tort claims before someone files a case against them. With some exceptions, the plaintiff must send a written claim to the ski resort operator about an injury at the ski area by registered or certified mail within 180 days of the injury or the date when the skier first knew or should have realized he or she was injured. With some exceptions, bars and taverns and people who have served liquor to intoxicated persons at private parties are entitled to written notice within 180 days of an injury to someone caused by an intoxicated person who was served at the bar or tavern or by a social host.

Defendants in contract disputes in some cases are entitled to alternatives to lawsuits. For example, a written contract may say that the parties to the contract must try to mediate or arbitrate their disputes rather than go to court. This requirement is typical in real estate deals, construction contracts, credit card agreements, and many consumer contracts. While mediation may cost little or nothing, arbitration can be quite expensive. Get legal advice about your particular situation before agreeing to arbitrate and before filing a claim against the seller or financer in small claims court. If you are planning to sue a contractor for a problem related to home construction or remodeling, see Chapter 8 for more guidance.

Where to file your case

To know where to file your case, you need to know about **jurisdiction** and **venue**. A case must have some connection with the state before Oregon can claim jurisdiction. If you are not sure whether your claim can be raised in an Oregon court, get some legal advice before you file.

If you know that Oregon is the right state in which to file the case, then you must decide the county (venue) in which it should be filed. As a general rule, the case can be filed in any county in which a defendant, or one of the defendants, lives or happens to be at the time the case starts. In the case of a tort, the case can start in the county where one of the defendants is or where the harm occurred.

Here are a few examples:

You were in a traffic accident in Utah involving a Utah driver. Even though you are licensed in Oregon, a court in Oregon will not have the authority (jurisdiction) to hear the case.

You were in a traffic accident in Morrow County caused by a Harney County driver. You can file your case in Morrow or Harney County.

You rented a house in Roseburg from a landlord who lives in Los Angeles. The landlord won't return your security deposit. For a claim based on contract, you file the case where one of the defendants is or lives, or in the county where the defendant was to perform the duty (in this case, in Douglas County). A landlord-tenant agreement is a contract. Thus, you can sue in Douglas County or Los Angeles for the return of a wrongfully held security deposit.

You live in Klamath Falls and you bought a brand new but unreasonably dangerous or defective product there that was manufactured in Salvador by a Delaware company. You can sue in Klamath County because the company is doing business in the county by having things for sale there.

SAMPLE attempt to settle—defective product

(your mailing address)

THE DATE of the letter—very important

Defendant's name
Defendant's mailing address

Re defective ceiling fan

Dear [defendant's name]:

Last month, I bought a ceiling fan at your store for $137. I took it home and paid an electrician $87.50 to install it. It did not work. The electrician said that there appeared to be a problem with the motor, and took the fan down at my request.

I brought the fan back to the store, and asked for my money back. You said you would repair or, if repair was impossible, replace the fan but not give me back my money. You said the fan would be ready within five days. When I called three weeks ago to see if the fan was ready, you said it was not and asked me to call back in a week. When I called two weeks ago, the fan still was not ready. This week when I called, someone else took a message and you have not called back.

It is now mid-summer and I need the fan badly, as my home is very hot. Please have a working fan ready for me to pick up by [specific date], or refund my money and the cost of the electrician. You can reach me at [phone number], or send my refund of $224.50 to the above address. I look forward to hearing from you.

Sincerely, [your name]

Enclosed—copy of receipt for purchase of fan; copy of electrician's bill

SAMPLE attempt to settle—security deposit request

[your address]
[date of letter]

[Defendant's name] [Defendant's address]
Re return of my security deposit

Dear [defendant's name]:

This letter follows my telephone call to you of yesterday, [date of call]. I called to find out why you had not returned my security deposit of $650 after I moved out two months ago. You stated that you sent part of the money, $200, to my current address two weeks ago.

Obviously, I have not received the money. Furthermore, I have not received an itemized statement explaining why you kept $450 when I left my apartment immaculate and in good condition. Under Oregon Revised Statute 90.300, you had 31 days in which to return my deposit or an explanation why you needed the money to fix any problem with the rental that I caused. You admitted that you did not send the money or any notice timely.

If I have to sue for the return of my money, the law will entitle me to double the amount wrongfully withheld. To avoid that, please return my $650 within the next [number] days, or no later than [specific date that many days in the future], to the address above. I look forward to receiving your check.

Thanks for your prompt attention.

Sincerely,

[your name]

CHAPTER 3

The plaintiff's claim

A small claims court case starts with filing a complaint (or **claim**) at a court clerk's office. The defendant is entitled to prompt formal notice that the plaintiff has filed a case against him or her.

Circuit court small claims

There are several ways to get the claim forms for a circuit court small claims case, and two ways to file your case. You can get the forms from the court clerk's office, you can download forms from the circuit court in the county where you will file your case, or you can get forms acceptable in all circuit court small claims cases by going online to www.courts.oregon.gov/OJD/forms/Pages/SmallClaims.aspx

Once you have the forms, you can file them by mail or in person. Or you can "e-file" them online so long as (1) you have an email address, (2) you can create PDF or PDF-A text-searchable documents, and (3) you are paying filing fees by credit or debit card. If you don't have a card or if you want to waive or defer your fees, you can work with the court directly, using paper documents. If you are a defendant, you can file your answer electronically, so long as you meet the three requirements above. You can still file paper documents at the courthouse. Only lawyers are required to file case documents electronically.

To file electronically, go to the Oregon Judicial Department i-Forms page: www.courts.oregon.gov/OJD/OnlineServices/iForms/Pages/index.aspx

There is a "Guide and File" questionnaire that will ask you about your case and will fill in blanks in the claim form.

For small claims departments in circuit courts, an increasing number of standard statewide forms is available. They include agreements of the parties to settle their case, notice of violation of an agreement to settle a case, motions for default judgment, and more. To see the full assortment, go to: www.courts. oregon.gov/OJD/forms/Pages/SmallClaims.aspx

Note that some counties may have even more forms for use in their own jurisdictions. On the State of Oregon courts homepage, find the county where your case is or will be filed and look there for those forms. A few counties have helpful written instructions, too.

Justice court small claims

Justice courts use paper case files. You cannot (yet, anyway) e-file there. Unlike circuit court small claims departments, justice courts do not have to accept the standard forms. Nor do justice courts necessarily put their own forms online, so a phone call or a letter may be needed just to be able to get the claim form you need. Keep in mind that such things as getting the right forms (and then getting them right!) can take time—and delay could mean missing your filing deadline.

Justice courts present one more challenge: a person who files a claim in justice court small claims must appear in person or have someone else appear in person on their behalf to file the court papers. Defendants can file their answers by mail.

Completing the forms

At the end of this chapter are examples of claims using a standard court form. The form has four parts:

- The *heading* shows the court where you are filing the case;
- The *caption* shows the names and contact information of the parties;
- The *body* describes the claim;
- The *signature line*, where the plaintiff signs his or her name and declares that the information in the claim is true

Some people feel intimidated about describing their claim, afraid they will not be able to "say it right." Looking at the examples should reassure you that you just need to keep it simple.

Not all claim forms give the plaintiff the option of asking for the return of property; they may simply say that the defendant owes the plaintiff money. You need to change the form if you want to make clear that you want your possession back. If the defendant does not intend to give back your property ("I sold it on e-Bay." "My ex-wife broke it over my head." "My dog ate your homework."), you still will want to ask for money to reimburse you for your loss. See an example at the end of this chapter.

The claim form requires the plaintiff to state that he or she has made an effort to collect the debt before filing the case. Do not file your case unless you have made the required effort to collect the debt and will be able to describe in court what the effort was. As described in Chapter 2, the court has the right not to hear your case if you cannot show that you attempted to resolve the problem before taking this step.

Interpreters and accommodations for disabilities

A plaintiff who has trouble speaking or understanding English has the right to a court interpreter. If you or any of your witnesses need an interpreter, ask the court clerk for one when you file your case. Likewise, if you or any of your witnesses need an American Sign Language signer or a voice amplifier, alert the clerk. (Court interpreters are highly trained and certified to work in the courtroom. You can't use a friend or family member who is not court-certified.)

In a few cases, a party in a small claims case may be homebound, in the hospital, or otherwise completely unable to come to the courthouse. Depending on what kinds of evidence are needed in the case, it may be possible to "appear" by telephone. In very rare instances (I know of two in 30 years), a judge and the other party have gone to the home, hospital, or facility in order to have a face-to-face hearing. To accommodate a serious health problem, the clerk's office needs to know about the issue immediately. Look for more information later in this chapter about appearing in person, appearing by phone, and getting a hearing postponed.

A word about court clerks

The court clerk's office is the link between the judge and the people who must use the court services. The law allows the court clerk to give general information about court procedures. The law does not allow court clerks to give legal advice—that is, information tailored specifically to a person's case. You will most likely work with an office where staff are allowed to provide enough information to help you understand the system and get your case underway. Most clerks can be enormously helpful if they are given the opportunity—so long as you don't expect specific legal advice.

In some court clerk offices, unfortunately, the policy is to give you no information at all—just to "be on the safe side." If you have to deal with a clerk in this kind of office, your experience may be unpleasant and frustrating. Remember that the staff are simply following the policy in the office. They don't like it any more than you do, so resist the urge to yell at them.

Costs associated with small claims

Before you can file your claim, you will want to know how much it will cost to file. Unfortunately, the only way to find out is to call the court where you intend to file the case or read the online fee schedule—the fee varies from county to county. And it may even vary in a single county based on the amount of your claim. (See Appendix C for a list of courts and their contact information.) In some counties, the fee covers the cost of court-sponsored pre-trial mediation as well as the cost of hearing your claim.

All courts accept cash and checks; some accept money orders, and some take Visa and Mastercard credit and debit cards. Checks to small claims departments of circuit courts should be made out to the State of Oregon. How justice courts want the check made out will vary from court to court. Remembering that your time limit may not allow for "do-overs," find out what your court requires before you file.

If you can't afford the filing fee

What if you don't have enough money to be able to file your case or to respond to a case filed against you? The United States Supreme Court has said that no one should be barred from getting the benefit of the courts simply because the person is living in poverty. The Oregon Supreme Court created standards to allow people with very low incomes and few assets to file and respond to cases without having to pay all or part of the fee at the time of filing. The court has the authority to determine whether to **waive** or **defer** all or part of the fees related to filing your case. If the court waives the fees, you will have no duty to pay those fees in the future. If the court gives you a **fee deferral,** you will have to pay the fees at a later time unless, after your trial, the judge orders the other party to pay the fees.

You can get waiver and deferral application forms from the courthouse or the individual court website. You will notice that the application form breaks down the costs of the case, such as the filing fee, service by a sheriff in Oregon, and a hearing fee. Be sure to mark all the categories for which you want a waiver or a deferral. Note: An Oregon fee waiver or deferral will not eliminate the cost of the delivery of court papers outside this state.

Complete the application form and sign it. Also fill out the caption of the order you want the judge to sign to waive or defer the fees. You may need to show proof of your inability to pay. Submit the forms, and any proof the court requires, along with your small claims court claim form. Ask the clerk when and where you should call to find out if a judge has granted your request. Note that the fee deferral and waiver procedure is not the same in all courts. Check the Supplemental Local Rules (SLR) in the county where you plan to file for more specific instruction.

Justice courts do not have to use the standard state form. But justice courts have to allow low-income plaintiffs and defendants to apply for waivers or deferrals of filing fees.

Warning: In a telephone survey, one circuit court small claims department said it would grant fee waivers or deferrals to defendants, but not to plaintiffs. This policy violates the constitutional right of low-income plaintiffs to get access to courts. A justice court clerk said that the court did not offer fee waivers or deferrals at all, even though state law requires all courts to provide waivers and deferrals for those who cannot afford to pay the filing fee. Get legal advice if a clerk refuses to allow you to ask for a fee waiver or deferral.

Filing your claim

When you file your claim in either the circuit court small claims department or in justice court, the court clerk gives the case a unique number. Be sure to keep the number for future reference. If you request a filing fee waiver or deferral, the case number may not be assigned until after a judge has approved the waiver or deferral. If the judge does not approve that request, the small claims case does not get filed until the plaintiff can come up with the filing fee. (In very rare cases, a judge will reject a request for a waiver from someone who is obviously eligible for it. If you have that experience, contact your local legal aid office or other attorney as soon as possible.) When the clerk accepts the case for filing, you will receive written instructions on how to notify the defendant. The clerk also completes a notice form for the defendant, which the plaintiff must arrange to deliver to the defendant along with a copy of the plaintiff's claim.

Serving the court papers on the defendant

Now that you have filed your claim, you need to arrange for the defendant to get official notice of the case. Giving this notice is called **service** or **service of process.** From reading Chapter 2, you know that if you are suing registered businesses or corporations, you will serve the registered agent for the business. The information in this section will explain how to serve an individual defendant.

You've done your homework (see Chapter 2), so you know where to find the defendant—if the defendant can be found. Even if you've been unable to locate the defendant, you still need to know this information because you will have to follow some of the same steps to prove to the court that you have made every reasonable effort to give notice.

If you file your case in the small claims department of circuit court, you can choose among several ways to have the papers served on the defendant. If one way is unsuccessful, you will have to try other methods. The first method is by certified mail, restricted delivery, return receipt. If you use this method, you must send a copy of your claim and a blank "defendant's notice of election" form to the defendant, at his or her last-known mailing address. The envelope must be marked "Return Receipt Requested" and "Deliver to Addressee Only." (Do not throw away any documentation from the post office showing that you tried to serve the papers this way!) When the defendant signs for the papers, the post office will send you the receipt, showing the date that the defendant signed for the papers. Look carefully at the receipt to make sure that it contains the defendant's signature; if someone else signed the receipt, you haven't met the legal requirement of serving the defendant. Fourteen days after the date the defendant signed for the papers, you can contact the court clerk to find out if the defendant has responded to your claim.

For a variety of reasons, the defendant may not receive—or may not sign for—the certified letter. In that case, you will have to try to give notice in a different way--by **personal service**. Personal service means that someone— not you—hands the papers to the defendant. Many plaintiffs opt to have a sheriff serve the papers this way, but any competent person who is at least 18 years old and has no stake in the outcome of the case can do this job.

If your case is filed in justice court, you must first try to use personal service. If personal service doesn't work, get legal advice about other options.

Using the sheriff to serve an individual

If you decide to have an Oregon sheriff deliver the court papers to the defendant, there is a minimum fee of $45 for up to two defendants per address, unless the court allows you to defer or waive that fee. For a round trip of 75 miles from the courthouse to the place of service, the sheriff can charge up to $45 more. A sheriff's department can serve papers only in its own county.

You will need to send the sheriff service fee to the county where you file your case if that's where the defendant is. The sheriff's office and the court are different agencies, so you will have to write separate checks for each. If the defendant is in another county, you will need to get copies from the court clerk of the papers to be served; and send those with your payment (or copy of fee waiver) to the sheriff's department in the other county, with as much identifying information as you can provide.

If you use a sheriff, a marshal, or a constable in another state to serve the papers, you will need to contact the agency in that state to find out what its costs and procedures are. (Ask, too, how long it usually takes the agency to serve the papers; in some places, it can take months. You may want to use a professional process server instead. Online and in the phone book they can be found under "legal messenger services" and "process servers." See more information about private process servers below.)

It is enormously helpful to the sheriff (or to any process server who doesn't know the defendant) if you can provide a physical description of the defendant or other information that will identify the person or the person's likely whereabouts (such as "starts drinking at the Elbow Room in Estacada at 10 a.m. daily" or "walks honey-colored cocker spaniel in Mt. Tabor Park every Saturday between 7 and 8 a.m.," "has the name Rosie tattooed on his right bicep" or "has cauliflower ear on her left side"). Providing a photo helps, too.

After serving the court papers on the defendant, the sheriff sends a **return of service** (also called an **affidavit of service, proof of service,** or a **certificate of service**) either to the court or to you. The return will say when the sheriff served the papers. This date is important, because after that date the defendant has 14 days to respond to the claim. If the sheriff sends it to you directly, make a copy for yourself and send the original to the court clerk right away. Until the clerk receives the original return of service, the case will not go forward. If the sheriff's office can't find the defendant within a reasonable time, it will notify you that its attempt to serve was unsuccessful. Keep the notice as proof that you tried; you may need it later.

Using a private server to serve an individual

You may need or want someone other than a sheriff to serve the papers. A trustworthy friend or family member can do the job if he or she is over 18. Or you may want to hire a professional process server, especially if you are suing someone who lives in another state where the sheriff or other official agency is so short-staffed that it can take several months to serve papers. Either way, the server will need to complete a **return of service** (also called **proof of service**) form after serving the papers on the defendant, then sign it before a notary, and return it to you so you can note the service date, make a copy of the form for your records, and then send the original to the court. You will have to provide the return of service form to any server who is not a law enforcement official. If this server can't find the defendant, he or she should write down what was done—and when--to try to locate the defendant, sign that writing before a notary, and send it to you.

Other methods of service on individuals

If you have been unable to serve the defendant by certified mail or by personal service in a circuit court small claims case, there are other ways in which to follow up. They range from free to cheap to expensive. "Expensive" may be more than the amount of your claim, so take that cost into account when deciding how strong your claim is.

If you are sure you know where the defendant lives, you can use **substitute service** if the defendant has avoided certified mail or personal service. The person who serves the papers can deliver them to anyone over age 14 at the defendant's home; the person who delivers the papers signs a notarized certificate of service that says when, where, and to whom the server delivered the papers. (That means that the server will have to find out the name—and sometimes the age--of the person to whom he or she gives the papers.) Then you must mail another copy of the notice of claim and defendant's notice of election to the defendant at the same address and on the same day. With the copy you must include a notarized statement that the copy that is mailed is an exact copy of the original claim and notice. (The notarized statement may be on the back of the copy of the claim form.) Once you've done the follow-up mailing, you need to complete another affidavit; this one tells the court when, and to whom, and the address to which you mailed the second copy of the papers. The 14-day waiting period begins the day after you send the follow-up mailing.

Another type of substitute service is **office service**, which you can use to serve someone who operates a business. The person who serves the papers must deliver them during regular business hours to whoever seems to be in charge. The server must find out the name of the person in charge, then complete a certificate of service, signing before a notary. Then, as you would do for substitute service, you mail a second set of the papers to the defendant at the business (or home, if you know it) address. You must then complete an affidavit of mailing that you turn in to the court along with the proof of service signed by the server. The 14-day waiting period begins the day after you send the follow- up mailing.

Service by publication

If none of the other ways to serve the defendant worked, you may have to resort to serving by publication or posting. **Service by publication** means that you have a newspaper of general circulation print a copy of the claim and notice to the defendant in its "Legal Notices" section once a week for four weeks. The newspaper must be in the county where the claim is filed, or, if you believe the defendant may be somewhere outside the county, in the county where the claim is filed *and* in the county where you believe the defendant is most likely to be found. Publication is expensive. Even if you have obtained a filing fee waiver from the court, you must pay in full and in advance for publication. Once 30 days have passed after the first date of publication, however, you can proceed with your case.

Not only is this process expensive; it also requires permission from the court. To get permission, you must file a **motion** asking to be allowed to publish, along with an affidavit that lays out all of the things you've done to try to find the defendant in order to give him or her notice of your case.

What is a newspaper of general circulation? In most communities, it's a daily newspaper to which any member of the public has access. In places where there is no daily newspaper, it is any weekly or more frequent newspaper available to the public that contains legal notices in its classified advertising section. If you have a choice of newspapers that qualify, check with them all to find out their rates—the cost can vary significantly.

Service by posting

A less expensive option is to file a motion and affidavit asking the court to allow you to have the claim and notice posted (generally at the courthouse) on a public bulletin board. While service by publication is costly and not very likely actually to alert someone that he or she is defendant, a courthouse bulletin board announcement is even less likely to make a defendant aware of the lawsuit. For that reason, almost all judges are reluctant to allow posting, and some judges never allow it.

Effect of service by publication or posting

A defendant who is served only by publication or posting may be excused from the time limit in which to respond, even after the plaintiff has obtained a judgment. The defendant needs to show lack of knowledge about the suit and any other good reason he or she has for not having responded sooner. A defendant may be able to reopen the case for up to a year after the plaintiff won it. If the defendant wins the reopened case, the plaintiff may have to give back anything collected from the defendant after getting the original judgment.

After the defendant has been served

After you learn that the defendant has received the court papers, send proof of the service to the court clerk's office. If the defendant was served by certified mail, make a copy of the signed return receipt and send the original to the court clerk. If the sheriff's office served the papers, it will usually send its certificate of service directly to the court clerk. The sheriff should send a copy of the form to you.

If an adult friend, family member, or professional process server served the papers, he or she will need to complete the certificate of service form before a notary and give you the form. An example of a proof of service form is at the end of this chapter. Make a copy of it for your records, and send the original to the court clerk. If you do not send this proof, the court will not schedule your hearing.

The return receipt or the certificate of service will show the date on which the defendant received the papers. Allow 14 days after that date to pass. Then wait a couple of days more, so that if the court received anything from the defendant it will have had time to process the paperwork. Call the court clerk to see if there has been a response. Be sure to tell the clerk the case number as well as the names of the parties.

If you had to serve by publication in a newspaper, at the end of the four- week publication period the newspaper will send you a form (called either an affidavit or a declaration) verifying that it published the notice of claim four times weekly. Submit that notice to the court clerk's office as your proof of service.

If the defendant doesn't respond

If the defendant doesn't file a response within the time allowed by law, you can now apply for a **default judgment** on the court form for that purpose. See www.courts.oregon.gov/OJD/docs/CivilSmallClaims/SC-Default-MotionStatus-Decl.pdf. You can mail or deliver this form to the court clerk. You will not have to prepare for a hearing; you will win the case automatically. If you obtained a fee deferral in order to file, be sure to remind the clerk (preferably in writing) that the balance of the filing fee still due to the court should become part of the judgment against the defendant.

If the defendant responds

You may hear from the defendant before the deadline for his or her official response to the court. He or she may want to pay off at least part of the amount you claim or to return property that belongs to you. If the defendant agrees to do, and actually does do, what you want before trial day, you have a duty to call off the trial by voluntarily dismissing your case. Call the court clerk's office as soon as you settle the problem, and follow up with a letter asking for dismissal.

If the defendant files a **Defendant's Notice of Election** or **Answer** denying your claim, the defendant must pay fees to respond to the claim and to get a trial.

The fees for defendants vary by county, too. Defendants also are eligible for fee waivers and deferrals based on poverty. See Chapter 4 for more information.

The defendant may respond with a denial that you are entitled to anything, in which case you will need to start preparing to prove your case at trial. The defendant may respond with a counterclaim. If so, you will need to consider how strong his or her claim is against you, especially if the counterclaim is for a larger amount of money than your claim is. You may want to give more thought to negotiating a solution informally, a solution that minimizes your risk in court. Note: Once the defendant has filed an answer/denial in the case, settling out of court before trial means that neither side will be eligible to get the court to award costs from the other party.

In some cases, the defendant will ask for the case to be transferred to circuit court. Businesses being sued by individuals sometimes do this to discourage the plaintiff from going forward with the case. If you are determined to follow through, you need to know that once a defendant asks for a transfer, you have only 20 days in which to re-file the case, in the form of a new, formal complaint, in circuit court. If you do not re-file within that time, your case will be dismissed. (In justice court, the time limit is only 10 days from the time the justice court transfers the case to circuit court.)

Re-filing in circuit court is not easy. You cannot just use the same forms that worked in small claims court. In fact, there are no standard forms for circuit court cases. You may need help drafting your complaint and other documents, and should seriously consider seeking the advice of, or representation by, an attorney. (See Appendix B, Resources, for some sources of help.) Like you, the defendant has the right to hire a lawyer in a circuit court case.

You will need to pay a new filing fee for the circuit court case, or get a new fee waiver or deferral. The case will likely have to go through court-supervised arbitration, another expense.

On the other hand, once you file in circuit court, there is no artificial limit on the amount of money you can claim. You will have more time to prepare your case, as regular cases move quite slowly. If you go ahead without an attorney, be ready to spend a lot of time doing legal research and drafting documents. Be ready to follow the various rules that apply to circuit court (ORCP, UTCR, the rules of evidence, and SLR). If you have access to a public law library, it will have useful manuals and other guides to help you. The Oregon State Bar books listed in Appendix B are some of the materials at law libraries to aid your case. Remember that librarians, just like court clerks, can't offer legal advice.

SAMPLE claim form—circuit court for money

IN THE CIRCUIT COURT OF THE STATE OF OREGON
FOR THE COUNTY OF _____
Small Claims Department

_____

_____
Plaintiff

(Inmate SID #, if applicable, _____)
v.

_____

_____
Defendant
☐Defendant is a public body

Case No: _____

**SMALL CLAIM AND
NOTICE OF SMALL CLAIM**

Filing fee at ORS 46.570

PLAINTIFF (☐Additional on attached page)

Name
_____

Street
_____

City / State / Zip
_____

Phone _____ County

DEFENDANT (☐Additional on attached page)

Name (enter Registered Agent, if necessary, on next page)
_____

Street (do not use a P.O. Box)
_____

City / State / Zip
_____

Phone _____ County

I, Plaintiff, claim that on or about *(date)*_____, the above-named defendants owed me the sum of (or property valued at) $_____ because _____

_____

_____

_____

_____

_____

_____

_____

_____, and this amount is still due.

I have paid (or will pay) :

    filing fees of $_____

    and service costs of $_____

Claim	$_____
+ Fees	$_____
+Costs	$_____
TOTAL	$_____

DECLARATION OF GOOD FAITH EFFORT

I, Plaintiff, have made a good faith effort to collect this claim from the defendants before filing this claim with the court clerk.

*(Describe your efforts):*_____

_____

_____

I hereby declare that the above statements are true to the best of my knowledge and belief. I understand they are made for use in court and I am subject to penalty for perjury.

_____   _____
Date   Plaintiff Signature

                                                _____
                                                Plaintiff Name (print)

DEFENDANT'S REGISTERED AGENT:

_____
Name

_____
Street (do not use a P.O. Box)

_____
City / State / Zip

_____
Phone   County

NOTICE TO DEFENDANT:
READ THESE PAPERS CAREFULLY!

Within **14 DAYS*** after receiving this notice you *MUST* do *ONE* of the following things in writing:

- Pay the claim plus filing fees and service expenses paid by plaintiff (send payment directly to the plaintiff, not to the court) **OR**
- Demand a hearing and pay the fee required (below) **OR**
- Demand a jury trial and pay the fee required (below). This option is available **only** if amount claimed is more than $750.

If you fail to do one of the above within 14 DAYS* after you get this notice, the plaintiff may ask the court to enter a judgment against you. The judgment will be for the amount of the claim, plus filing fees and service costs paid by the plaintiff, plus a prevailing party fee. If you are not able to respond in time because you are in active military service of the United States, talk to a legal advisor about the Servicemembers Civil Relief Act.

COURT NAME / ADDRESS / PHONE #
>
>
>

Defendant's Filing Fees *(must be filled in by the PLAINTIFF)*:

(1) To demand a hearing if the amount claimed is $2,500 or less $ _____
(2) To demand a hearing if the amount claimed is more than $2,500 $ _____
(3) To demand a jury trial (only if amount claimed is over $750) $ _____

You can fill out and file your *Response* online at *www.courts.oregon.gov/iforms*. If you have questions about filing procedures, go to *www.courts.oregon.gov*. Or you may contact the court clerk. The clerk *cannot* give you legal advice about the claim.

*NOTE: If the plaintiff is an <u>inmate</u> (ORS 30.642) AND the defendant is a <u>government agency or other public body</u> (ORS 30.260), the defendant must respond within **30 days** after receiving this Notice.

Small Claim and Notice of Small Claim
Page **3** of **3**

Case No: _____
(Dec 2017)

SAMPLE claim form—justice court for delivery of items under contract

IN THE JUSTICE COURT OF THE STATE OF OREGON
FOR THE COUNTY OF TILLAMOOK

My full name) Plaintiff(s) name) **My street address and P.O. Box, if any**) Address (physical & mailing)) **My town, state, zip and phone number**) City, State, Zip, Phone)))) **Linda Loomis and Scott Hagle DBA**) Defendant name) **The Wedding Man**) Defendant name) **Street address and P.O. Box, if any**) Address (physical & mailing)) **Their town, state, zip and phone**) City, State, Zip Phone)	Case No. _____ **SMALL CLAIM and** **NOTICE OF CLAIM**

I, plaintiff, claim that on or about **May 12, 2018,** the above named defendant(s) owed me the sum of **wedding photographs from April 1, 2018 or the cost of the photos** and this sum is still owing. The nature of the claim is as follows: **Defendants contracted for $600 to take wedding pictures, then never delivered the pictures.**

STATE OF OREGON)
TILLAMOOK COUNTY) ss

I, plaintiff, state that I have made the above claim and that it is true as I verily believe. I further certify that I have made a bona fide effort to collect this claim prior to filing.

Subscribed before me this _____ day of _____, _____.

Plaintiff signature_____

Notary/Clerk_____

****

I certify that the foregoing is a true copy of the claim filed.
Clerk_____

****

NOTICE TO DEFENDANT [part of form but not included as part of sample]

SAMPLE Certificate of Service

IN THE CIRCUIT COURT OF THE STATE OR OREGON
FOR THE COUNTY OF _____
SMALL CLAIMS DEPARTMENT

_____)
Plaintiff/s   )   Case No: _____
vs   )
)
_____)
Defendant/s   )   CERTIFICATE OF SERVICE
)   BY PERSONAL SERVICE

I, _____, HEREBY CERTIFY that I am resident of the County of _____, State of _____. I am a competent person over the age of 18 years and I not a party to nor an attorney in this proceeding. I certify that the person, firm, or corporation served is the identical one named in this action.

On the ____ day of _____, 20___, at _____ a.m./p.m., I personally served a true copy of Small Claim and Notice of Claim by delivering them to the defendant, _____, at the following address: _____, in the County of _____, in the State of _____ .

Certificate of Document Preparation. You are required to truthfully complete this certificate regarding the document you are filing with the court. Check all boxes and complete all blanks that apply:

☐   I selected this document for myself and I completed it without paid assistance.
☐   I paid or will pay money to _____ for assistance in preparing this form.

I hereby declare that the above statement is true to the best of my knowledge and belief, and that I understand it is made for use as evidence in court and is subject to penalty for perjury

Dated this _____ day of _____, 20____

_____

Signature of Server   Print Name

_____

Address or Contact Address   City, State, Zip   Phone or Contact Phone

48

CHAPTER 4

Defending yourself in a small claims case

How you know you're being sued

Usually, you find out when you get court papers. How do court papers come to you? They can be **served** in one of several ways. An adult who is not the plaintiff can hand them to you. The plaintiff can mail them to you by certified mail with restricted delivery and request a return receipt from the post office. If you have a business that is being sued, the papers may come to your office or store, or to someone you designated as your agent for service when you registered your business or corporation with the Oregon Secretary of State. The papers can be delivered to someone over age 14 at your home, with a copy mailed by regular mail. These are the most common methods, but there are others as well, as outlined in Chapter 3.

So now what? Humans have a long history of ignoring problems, hoping they will go away. Enough problems do go away to make this problem-solving strategy seem like a pretty good one for some things. Unfortunately, it's a really bad strategy to use in response to being served court papers. When someone hands you the papers—a copy of a **summons and complaint** in a circuit court case, or, in a small claims case, the **claim and notice of claim** filed by the plaintiff—it does you no good to refuse to "accept" them. Throwing the papers away without reading them or leaving them on the seat of your car without looking at them won't keep the court from making a decision that affects your rights. *It is always a mistake to ignore a document that is an official paper issued by a lawyer or a court.* People who have done so have later discovered things such as that their credit rating has been destroyed, their paycheck has been garnished, there is a lien on their property, the sheriff has come to move all of their belongings out of their rental, their home is being foreclosed on, or—in some cases—a judge has issued a bench warrant for them to be brought into court by the police! In short, read the papers. You can't make an intelligent decision until you do.

When there's no legal defense

Let's look at a typical small claims case to see what can happen. In this example, a collection agency claims you owe it $1,000 plus interest. You read the claim, and, feeling a little sick, shrug, "Yes, that's true. I've owed the money since last year, but I am unable to pay it." Not being able to pay isn't a legal **defense** to a legitimate debt. Unless there are other facts to complicate the case (keep reading for an example), if you go to court to fight the claim you will lose the case—*and* the fee you paid to file your answer, *and* the plaintiff's filing fees and court costs, *and* the **prevailing party fee**. So it probably doesn't make sense for you to file an answer in this case. (Exceptions exist. See Notes 1 and 2 below.) You decide not to appear in court. The plaintiff will win the case by **default**.

What happens next? The court will enter a judgment against you for the amount the plaintiff claimed, and for the plaintiff's court costs and fees. Would the result have been any different if you had gone to court? No. The plaintiff was going to win no matter what. By not filing an answer to fight against a valid debt, you saved a little time and some money by not paying your own filing fee.

Note 1: There are a few other considerations you may want to take into account. One is that filing a defendant's election for a trial gives you more time to save up a payment if you want to try to pay off the claim before the plaintiff gets a judgment. It also gives you more time to negotiate a settlement. In both situations, if you settle out of court, you avoid getting hit with the prevailing party fee.

50

Note 2: If your case is in a county where the court offers pre-hearing mediation, it can sometimes be worth the risk of answering the complaint just to get the chance to try to negotiate terms of payment of the debt with a neutral party in the room to help you get there. A payment arrangement—one you can actually follow until the debt is paid in full—is usually preferable to giving the creditor the right to garnish your wages or bank account or business income. A court judgment against you gives the creditor that right, along with court-related fees added to the original debt.

When there is a legal defense

But what would happen if the facts were a little different? Suppose that the debt was from 27 years ago. Or that the collection agency had called you repeatedly to threaten you with violence or jail if you didn't pay. Or that you are quite certain that you are not the person the collection agency is after. In any of these situations, you might very well have some defenses or counterclaims that could reduce or even eliminate the plaintiff's claim against you. In these situations, it would probably be wise to ask for a trial. It would absolutely be wise to get advice from a lawyer. For some guidance on how to evaluate your chances in various kinds of cases, see Chapters 7, 8, and 9.

Before you respond

You are entitled to an opportunity to settle the dispute before the plaintiff files a court claim against you. If you get served court papers without any advance discussion or contact, you may have a defense against the small claims case: the plaintiff must state under oath when filing the case that efforts to settle were unsuccessful. Sometimes defendants get surprised in court when they raise that defense—because there is no strict rule about the timing of settlement efforts or even what constitutes an "effort". If a collection agency is suing you, for example, it may simply have sent you a series of letters demanding payment. Those count as efforts to settle. The most recent letter could have come to you six months before the agency filed suit. It still counts. No one has to come to you and say, "If we can't work this out in the next week, I am going to sue you in two weeks." (Exception: in consumer cases, a collection agency that does threaten an imminent lawsuit must in fact file court papers without waiting.) In addition, some judges disregard the plaintiff's failure to try to work out a solution to the problem outside of court: "If the parties are both here, I'm going to deal with their problem," says one judge.

As a practical matter, it's usually in your best interest to work out disputes informally. Debts can be negotiated and compromised; parties can establish payment plans, write off interest, and more. Taking advantage of free or low-cost mediation services is a good idea when those are available.

When is it *not* in your best interest to try to resolve problems before the plaintiff files? The short answer is when the plaintiff has a weak claim and you have a strong defense or a strong counterclaim or both.

Here are two examples of such situations:

1. You are a residential tenant who moved out after proper written notice one year and two weeks ago. At move-out, you took photos of the condition of the rental when you moved out. Two friends inspected the property, and pronounced it immaculate. You arranged for your mail to be forwarded to your new address, and you wrote a letter to your landlord to let her know where to return your security deposit. You made and kept a copy of that letter. The landlord has just sued you for damage to the rental. The landlord's case against you is very weak: first, there was no effort to settle. Second, the landlord had only one year after getting back possession of the rental in which to file a case against you for this kind of claim, and the year is up. She no longer has the right to sue you. Third, you have extensive proof, from photos and witnesses, that you left the rental in excellent condition. At the same time, you have a strong counterclaim against the landlord for the return of your security deposit. (Your time limit to sue for your security deposit is one year from the time the landlord should have sent you your deposit—31 days after you moved out.) You likely will win a judgment not only for your full deposit, but also for statutory damages, as well as your filing fee, court costs, and a prevailing party fee. (If the landlord is one who cheats people this way as a regular business practice, you may even have a claim for an unlawful trade practice in addition to your claims under the landlord-tenant act. Talk to a lawyer about this possibility.)

2. A collection agency wants to collect a valid consumer debt of $185 you incurred six months ago. It has sent you numerous letters demanding payment. You have been unable to pay, even though you want to. The

agency begins to call you repeatedly at home late at night without your permission, and it calls your job and tells your supervisor that you are a deadbeat. You write a letter to the agency demanding that it stop calling you and to stop calling your work, but it persists. Now it is suing you for the money, interest, and court fees. In this case, you do not have a defense to the debt itself, but you have counterclaims based on the agency's illegal conduct in trying to collect—unauthorized late night calls, contacts with third parties about your debt, telling third parties you are a deadbeat, refusing to stop contacting you when asked in writing to do so. You have strong proof of this illegal conduct—your roommate has answered some late-night phone calls, your boss knows what she heard from the collectors, you have a copy of the letter you sent asking the company to stop contacting you. The amount of your counterclaims (set by statute) will be higher than the agency's claim against you.

In both of these examples, it takes some knowledge of your legal rights under specific state or federal statutes to determine whether it makes sense to "play chicken" with the plaintiff, going to trial in the hope that the result will be that the plaintiff owes you money rather than the other way around. The bottom line: get legal advice as soon as possible, so you can make an informed decision about how to respond when sued.

The clock starts ticking

Now you have been served a copy of the court papers. As explained above, a defendant has only 14 days following the day he or she receives a copy of the plaintiff's claim to decide what to do in response. When you receive the claim, reach for your calendar and mark your deadline on it. (If you receive papers on May 1, May 15 is the deadline. If May 15 falls on Saturday, Sunday, or a court holiday, the next court business day is your deadline. If you are unsure whether a specific holiday is also a court holiday, check http://courts.oregon.gov/OJD/courts for a complete list.) The deadline date is the date by which the court must *receive* your response; if you mail your response, the postmark date doesn't count.

Once you know your timeframe, consider whether there is something you can do to resolve the problem. The law allows you and the plaintiff to keep talking about a solution all the way to the day of trial. Two big benefits of working out the problem before you have to file an answer is that you save the cost of the court filing fee, and the plaintiff must drop—**dismiss**—the case. You avoid the risk of having a judgment against you that would affect your credit score. Even if you can come to an agreement after you file your answer and pay your court fee, you still avoid the risk of a possible judgment against you.

Important: If you and the plaintiff come to an agreement, make sure the plaintiff follows through by dismissing the case. Dishonest plaintiffs have "settled", then gone on to get a judgment against the absent defendant who believes the case is over. Put any agreement in writing, make sure the plaintiff signs and dates it, and get receipts for any payment you make! Call the court clerk yourself to announce the settlement, and take, fax, or send (if there's enough time) a copy of the agreement to the clerk to be put in your case file.

If you're convinced that you and the plaintiff are not going to see eye to eye, then it's time to start getting ready to defend yourself. First, check the amount of the claim—if it's over $10,000, small claims court doesn't have jurisdiction to hear the case. Or, if you live outside Oregon and the facts leading to the case occurred outside Oregon (see Chapter 1 for a fuller description), it's possible that no Oregon court has jurisdiction. You will need to contact the court in writing, with a copy sent to the plaintiff, to ask it to dismiss the case against you and explaining your reason.

Next, find out which court is scheduled to hear the case. As described in Chapter 3, the plaintiff must file the case in the proper venue. If the plaintiff has picked a court in the wrong venue and you do not object immediately, you waive your right to object later. If the plaintiff filed in a wrong county that is reasonably convenient to you, however, you may decide that where to have the trial is not that important. And if you have no legal defense to the claim and you don't intend to fight it, getting the case into the proper venue doesn't matter.

Getting a change of venue

If you believe that the plaintiff has filed the case in the wrong venue, you can ask the judge in the case to transfer it to the right county. You do this by sending a letter to the judge no later than the time you file your notice of defendant's election and pay your filing fee or submit your request for a fee deferral or waiver. The letter should explain why you think the current venue is the wrong one, and which county you think should hear the case instead. See the example at the end of this chapter.

At the same time you send this objection to the court, you must also send a copy to the plaintiff. Keep a copy for your own records. After the plaintiff receives the letter, he or she has 14 days in which to respond to the court, explaining why the plaintiff thinks the first court is the right one. (In some courts, the court clerk sends a copy of your letter to the plaintiff, too, and starts the 14-day count then.) After waiting for 14 days for a response from the plaintiff, the court looks at the objection and decides whether the case belongs in a different county. The parties will be notified of the decision by letter. If the judge decides the case must be moved, the plaintiff may have to pay for a certification of the transfer; the cost of copies of the documents in the case file, at 25 cents per page; and the filing fee in the new county. The court clerk's office will explain what the plaintiff needs to do to get the case transferred. If the plaintiff received a fee waiver or deferral, he or she will have to seek a new one in the new county.

The plaintiff must re-file in the right county within 20 days after receiving the decision from the first court. If the plaintiff does not do so, the judge in the original county normally will dismiss the case and give you a judgment against the plaintiff for your court costs. If the judge in the original county concludes that it is the proper venue, the judge will have the court clerk schedule a hearing there; both parties will get written notice of their hearing date. Note: At least one justice court does not transfer the case when venue is improper; it simply dismisses the case, making the plaintiff file anew in the right county. For plaintiffs who file there at the last minute, this procedure could result in plaintiff's missing the statute of limitations.

Needless to say, the time when you are waiting for a decision or a court date is not a good time to head off on vacation. You may come home to find in your mail box the notice of a hearing date—that is now past. If you know you are going to be away during the time you would expect to get notice from the court about its decision or a hearing date, have someone monitor your mail, or ask in writing before you leave for the court to set the hearing after your planned date of return. Any request you send to the court you should also send to the plaintiff at the same time. The plaintiff may not agree to a **continuance** (postponement) of the hearing, but with advance notice the plaintiff is less likely to have a good reason not to postpone the hearing.

If you have a conflict with the hearing date

Plaintiffs and defendants both should know this:

If you have to work on the day set for your hearing, if it's your daughter's birthday or your wedding anniversary, a judge is likely not going to consider giving you a new hearing date. If, on the other hand, you are scheduled for a serious surgery on the day of your trial; if your office is moving to new quarters that day and you are in charge of the move; if your spouse is near death; if it's your wedding day; if you are the defendant and you bought pricey and nonrefundable, nontransferable tickets for a Caribbean cruise before you knew about this lawsuit—a judge is likely to be more sympathetic. If your reason to postpone the case is important, contact the court clerk immediately to explain the problem and ask for a continuance of the case. (The clerk may want a letter or an email in addition to your phone request; if so, fax or email a full explanation right away.) If your reason is simply that your day-to-day schedule makes going to court very inconvenient, you should prepare to fit your trial into your schedule if you really want your "day in court." As described above, make sure you notify the other side about the conflict as soon as you notify the court, and as soon as you possibly can, to improve your chances of getting a different court date.

If mediation is available

Your hearing notice should indicate whether the court has a small claims mediation or pre-trial settlement program. If it does, in most cases you should take advantage of it—especially if the plaintiff's case is fairly strong and you want to negotiate a payment plan or other settlement of the case. (One small claims clerk estimates that parties to small claims cases reach settlement in mediation in about 75 per cent of cases.) Decide what you think would be a fair resolution of the case, and prepare to present some alternatives to the "all or nothing" solution frequently dispensed in the courtroom. Participating in mediation also gives you an idea how strong the plaintiff's case is, if you don't already know, as well as what the plaintiff is likely to say in court.

If you prefer not to mediate, find out from the court clerk whether mediation is mandatory. If it is, you may not be able to continue to court without participating in it. Even if you must mediate, though, remember that you do not have to come to an agreement in mediation—you still have the right to take your case in front of a judge.

Responding to the claim

Are you in the right? Are you in the wrong? Do you have any defenses to the plaintiff's claim that would allow you to win the case? Do you have any counter- claims that would cause the plaintiff to become indebted to you? The answers to these questions will determine how you should respond to the claim. To get those answers, you will do well to get some competent legal advice and do some research into your legal rights. See Appendix B for ways to get started on this important step in making your decision. Then read Chapters 7, 8, and 9, "Making your case."

The range of options

The court papers you received include the "Defendant's Notice of Election" or answer—the form that you can send back to the court to tell it how you plan to respond to the plaintiff's claim. The form provides you with four choices:

- Admit the plaintiff's claim, and show written proof to the court within the 14-day response period that you have paid off the claim, including the plaintiff's court costs and service fees. It is essential to get the plaintiff's signature on this agreement, or show the cancelled check or receipt for the amount of the claim. (If you and the plaintiff settle the case for less than the full amount plaintiff would get, the plaintiff still can and should sign an agreement saying that the full debt has been paid off.)
- Deny the plaintiff's claim, and ask for a hearing
- Deny the plaintiff's claim, and raise a counterclaim
- Deny the plaintiff's claim, and, if the claim is for more than $750, ask

for a jury trial in circuit court.

If you want to make a counterclaim, know that, like the plaintiff's claim, it is limited to $10,000. If you ask for more, the judge will remove your claim from the case.

Asking for a jury trial in circuit court is sometimes a good idea, although you must pay additional court fees to do so. Many plaintiffs do not want to go through the additional trouble—delay and expenses, drafting a formal complaint, and following rules of evidence—and simply stop their cases, which are eventually dismissed. Obviously, if the plaintiff does file a claim in circuit court, you will have to defend your case following all the same rules that apply in circuit court.

You have one other choice that doesn't appear on the form: allow the plaintiff to get a default judgment against you. This option would mean that you send nothing back to the court. It is sometimes the right thing to do if you are certain you have no legal defense and no counterclaim, and if you are convinced that the plaintiff will not settle (in informal negotiation or mediation) for less than the full claim and you are unable to pay it off right now.

Doing your homework—fast

As a defendant, you have to work under two deadlines—the 14-day filing limit, and the trial date. For the first deadline, you need to determine how to respond to the plaintiff's claim. For the second one, you may need to conduct legal research. If you possibly can, you will want to observe at least one small claims or other trial session before your own trial date comes. (So many people handle small claims court so poorly that you may learn only what not to do in your own case.) You definitely need to gather evidence, find and prepare your witnesses to testify, and prepare your own testimony. How much time do you have to prepare for your hearing? That depends on where the case is filed. In larger counties with circuit court small claims departments, the parties can expect to wait five weeks to three months or even longer for their trial date. In some justice court districts, the trial can be set as soon as two weeks later. Court clerks can give you an estimate of how much time you have—but remember, it's only an estimate.

See Chapters 7, 8, and 9, "Making your case."

SAMPLE request for change of venue

Your address
The date of your letter

Name of court
Address

Re small claims case # (your case number), plaintiff's name v. defendant's name

Dear small claims clerk:

I write to ask for a change of venue in the above case, which I believe the plaintiff has filed in the wrong county. My reason(s) for asking for this change (is/are):

1. The plaintiff's claim is based on a traffic accident that occurred in Bend, Oregon.
2. Bend is located in Deschutes County.
3. I live in Deschutes County.
4. The plaintiff should not have filed this case in Crook County, which has no connection to the facts in our case.

I am sending a copy of this letter to the plaintiff.

Thank you for considering this request. I look forward to hearing from you.

Sincerely,

(your name)
(phone or email or both)

cc: (name of plaintiff)

CHAPTER 5

What to expect from judges

What judges do

If your ideas about small claims court come from watching TV court shows, you might think that a judge's primary goal in life is to interrupt people and humiliate them for 30 minutes at a time. Fortunately, the vast majority of judges in the real world aren't like that.

It is the job of a judge to sort through what the parties claim are the facts that give them the right to win the case; look at the laws that the parties say apply to their version of the facts; and then come to the decision that the law requires under the facts. This process isn't nearly as easy as it sounds. If it were, we could simply feed our facts into a computer, which would spit out a "decision." But judges look at not just what they are told, but also at whether some parties and witnesses are simply more believable. From time to time, they get fooled— just like other people.

Also unlike computers, judges must exercise discretion. They should have an understanding of the policy behind a particular law, and must determine whether a ruling that blindly follows the law flies in the face of the policy it was intended to further.

While trying to make a fair ruling, judges are under enormous pressure to handle a great number of cases in a very short period of time. Because of this time pressure (and because many people are not properly prepared to handle their case efficiently), judges sometimes may seem impatient. Keeping a judge's attention requires you to tell your side of the story clearly, quickly, and straightforwardly.

What judges know

What a judge knows about the law that applies to your case is obviously going to be important to the way the case turns out. Non-lawyers and new lawyers often assume that the judge will know more than they themselves do about the law that affects their cases. After all, most judges were lawyers for a decade or more before becoming judges. But anyone who has ever meandered through the thousands of volumes of books in any law library soon realizes that not even judges could master more than a small part of the vast array of laws.

Most judges have done just that—mastered a small part of the law. Many judges formerly were criminal prosecutors; they know a great deal about **criminal law** and procedure, but may have very little familiarity with **civil law**, the law that people rely on in small claims court cases. And some judges were in general private practice before they became judges. Those judges are likely to know about the rights of the "haves"—clients who have properties, businesses, and the money to hire lawyers. They are likely to know a great deal about the rights of creditors and insurance companies and debt collection agencies and landlords. These judges may have little or no experience with the rights of debtors, hourly workers, tenants, and consumers generally. For plaintiffs and defendants in small claims consumer and debt cases, the judge's lack of background in these areas of law means that the parties will need not only to present the facts of their cases but also educate the judge about the law and how to apply it to those facts.

You will likely not know the background of the judge before whom you will appear in any event; therefore, it is always a good idea to assume that the judge has no background in the law that applies to your case, no matter what kind it is, and prepare your case accordingly. A judge who has a good overall picture of the situation is much better equipped to make the right decision.

How judges see themselves

Like people in every other profession, no two judges approach their jobs in the same way. And, like everyone else, they come with their backgrounds and their prejudices. Despite struggling to be fair and objective, they aren't perfect. But they strive to be ethical, logical, and reasonable.

Judges have heard horrible things about human behavior in their time on the bench and before that in their time as lawyers. It's easy to become hardened to tragic events in the lives of those who must use the courts. Judges have to struggle to remain sensitive and to remember that a bad act, even one that may not be a crime, can still cause great harm.

Meanwhile, judges have to live with being the "movie stars" of the justice system. Lawyers—including lawyers who make much more money than judges do—treat them with great deference. As you might imagine, it's not easy to be humble when everyone is telling you how great you are. To their credit, most judges don't let their exalted status go to their heads. But they do expect to be treated with respect.

How judges see you

While it's true that judges bring their backgrounds and biases to work with them, how a judge will view you and your case is largely in your hands. You cannot expect "your" judge to advocate for you. As a party in a case, you have the job of being your own advocate; the judge has the job of deciding what happens to the claim that you make.

Most people go to court only as a last resort. Thus, when you file a lawsuit or when you commit to fight a claim made against you, you probably feel very wronged—violated and outraged. You may feel even more outraged if the judge in your case doesn't seem to feel passionate about your situation, too. But judges must remain impartial. What your judge will appreciate is a brief, clear presentation of the facts of your case and, if it's not obvious, an explanation of how the law applies.

Your judge will appreciate also that you bring the right attitude into the courtroom. There are two classic wrong ways to present yourself in court: one is to grovel before the judge like a beaten dog, expecting the judge to take up your side of the battle. The judge cannot do that. The other is to approach the experience as an exercise in "showing the judge who's boss." When a party tries to bully the judge, the other people in the courtroom are grinning and rolling their eyes—because they know who the boss in the courtroom is. A person who treats the judge badly is less likely to be trusted or believed—and therefore less likely to win his or her case. The judge will also notice how you treat the opposing party.

It's generally accepted that, if we look respectable, we *are* respectable. That's a stereotype that isn't true all that often, but it's certainly true that looking "respectable" is an easy way to project the message that we are respect*ful*. The person who appears in court wearing clean conservative clothing will get the benefit of the doubt. The person wearing a baseball hat and a wife-beater likely will not. (A quick trip to a second-hand store can make all the difference in how you are perceived.) It's unfortunate that how you look can make a difference, but taking up that crusade when you are trying to get something else from a court is the wrong way and the wrong place to get that point across.

"My judge isn't even a judge!"

In a few areas of Oregon, small claims are heard in justice court. An elected justice of the peace presides over the cases, and that person may or may not have a legal background. In that situation the law provides for limited appeal rights—something not available in small claims departments of the circuit court. See Chapter 12 for an explanation of those rights.

Avoiding the bad apples

Most judges do their very best to be fair and impartial. Some are heroic--from time to time, you hear about them on the news, as they uphold the law in the face of loud public criticism or pressure from unhappy officials. A few judges, however, are in the wrong job. You probably do not want to appear before one of them. You can't "shop" for a judge you think would do the best job on your case, but you can research whether there is a judge who shouldn't be allowed to handle your case.

Finding out about the quality of small claims judges may take some time. But if you want to find out, do so before you file your case if there's enough time; it may be too late once you file. If you know local lawyers who appear in court, they may tell you their opinion about the judges they see in action. If you spend time in a courtroom watching other people's cases, you may be able to figure out yourself if there's a judge to avoid. You can ask a court clerk which judges are most often **recused** from hearing cases, although the clerk may not know or may choose not to tell you. However, it's good to know that judges who are frequently recused (removed from hearing a case at the request of one of the lawyers on the case) are perceived to be biased, at least for certain kinds of cases.

Examples:

- A criminal defense attorney might believe that the judge, a former prosecutor, always sides with the prosecution rather than listening to the whole story.
- A person with a civil case believes that a certain judge will be unfair to him because the judge knew him to be the friend of someone the judge convicted of a serious crime.

Obviously, a judge who is routinely recused in certain kinds of cases may or may not be biased in reality. And a judge who is biased about one issue will likely not have a bias about other issues. It's a good idea to stay away from judges who have been recused by many lawyers in a variety of cases, however.

Getting a judge recused

A judge can be recused (or "disqualified") from hearing a case for a number of reasons. Sometimes judges even recuse themselves. It's their duty to do so if they

1. Have a personal interest in the case
2. Were not acting as the judge during the hearing of a case and are now being asked to make a decision in that case
3. Are related to any of the parties, or any of their attorneys, or work in the same law office as any of the attorneys in the case
4. Have been an attorney in the case at any time
5. Are asked to review in their role as appellate judges one of their own decisions made while they were trial judges

On occasion, a judge may not realize this apparent conflict of interest exists until everyone is at the hearing. In those cases, the judge will announce in court that he or she has one of the problems listed above. When that happens, a party concerned about whether the judge's relationship would jeopardize his or her case must **move** (make a formal request to the court) to disqualify the judge and have the hearing set in front of a different judge. Not to do so means that the party waives the right to have the case heard by someone else, with no recourse later on if he or she doesn't think the outcome of the case is fair.

Getting a different judge will mean the hearing likely will be scheduled for another date.

If you decide you do want a different judge based on this judge's disclosure about a possible conflict of interest, here's an example of what you might say: "Thank you, your honor, for making us aware of this. I respectfully request that our case get assigned to a different judge."

Normally, the notice from the court clerk telling you when your hearing is will also list the name of the judge who will hear the case. If the notice does not mention the name of the judge and you have good reason not to want a certain judge to hear the case, you can call the court clerk to find out. If the clerk does not know, it is best to file a **motion and affidavit** now anyway asking not to have your case assigned to that judge.

What constitutes a good reason to change judges? According to state law, it's the belief that a person cannot have a fair and impartial hearing by a specific judge. The belief must be sincere, however; it is not acceptable to ask for a different judge just to delay your court date.

How to get a different judge differs slightly among the courts. **Supplemental local court rules** can provide county-specific information. See www.ojd. state.or.us for specific courts. Some judicial districts, Multnomah County for example, require parties to ask for recusal as soon as the assignment to a judge is made. Under the Multnomah County rule, a party must at least orally notify the court clerk on the same day the party learns who the judge is to be; the formal motion and affidavit to recuse must be filed no later than the following business day. If the judge has made *any* decision in the case already (except for signing a filing fee waiver or deferral or a motion to extend time to file documents in a case), he or she cannot be recused. The parties in a case each have the right to up to two requests to recuse judges for good cause.

In judicial districts without a local rule on recusal, the time limit for filing a motion to recuse is different. In a **contested** case, the parties have a choice of times—(1) within ten days after their case has been assigned to a judge or up to five days after the setting of the trial date. There's a third time limit if the judge is coming from another county to hear the case—only up to five days after the party gets notice of the assignment to this judge. In these judicial districts, too, a motion to recuse will be honored only if the judge has made no decision in the case yet other than the two exceptions mentioned above.

If you decide you need to recuse a judge, what happens after you file your motion and affidavit to disqualify that judge? A different judge will review your request. Your request will be honored unless the original judge or the presiding judge of the district has a good reason to believe you are filing the request in bad faith and the judge can prove it at a hearing. It is very rare that the court will deny a motion to recuse a judge.

Complaining about a bad apple

What if you wind up with that rare judge who is obnoxious and unprofessional? You probably won't be able to do anything about the outcome of the case. You may even have *won* the case! Still, improper conduct can and should be reported to the Oregon Commission on Judicial Fitness and Disability. Remember: It is not the job of the Commission to resolve complaints about how a particular case turned out.

Contact information for the Commission is:

Oregon Commission on Judicial Fitness and Disability
P.O. Box 1130
Beaverton OR 97075
Phone: (503) 626-6776
Website address for more information: www.ojd.state.or.us/cjfd

The website explains in some detail what kinds of conduct should be reported to the Judicial Fitness Commission, and how the commission investigates complaints.

CHAPTER 6

Preparing Your Case for Trial

When you decide to go to court, it's important to be right. But it's just as important to be prepared. If you can't describe the facts simply and clearly so that a judge can quickly understand what happened, or if you don't provide proof for each element of your claim, you make it harder for the judge to rule your way. This chapter will prepare you to make your best case.

Explaining facts

Explaining facts clearly is not something we do very well day to day. Spend half an hour listening to people talk, and you will see them constantly asking each other questions about when, where, what was said, what was meant, who was there, etc. We are not accustomed to supplying all the facts because, in conversation, we are always helping each other complete the picture. In a courtroom, the judge doesn't get this help. The court relies on you to supply all the information it needs.

It's important to remember, too, that in a court case, you start out in a vacuum: nothing exists until someone, a party or other witness, says it does. That's why it's important to ensure that you present *all* the facts you need to prove your case.

Here's an example:

"My claim is for $3,250.00. Mr. Defendant's car rear-ended my car at a stop sign on Canyon Boulevard where it crosses West Main Street here in John Day. The accident occurred on March 12 of this year."

With these three sentences, you have:

- Explained that your case is within the small claims court's jurisdiction (because small claims court cannot handle cases worth more than $10,000);
- Established the proper venue (because you are in court in the county where the accident occurred);
- Explained how the claim arose (the accident); and
- Filed your case within the time limit the law allows.

These four things must be described in every case that the plaintiff or counter-claiming defendant presents. The fifth thing that you must explain is *why* you should get the amount of money (or the thing) you asked for. In the case above, you will provide at least one estimate for the cost of the car repair, or the bill for the repair if it's already been made.

Consider what the defendant may say—you will need to be ready to respond to it. You know this already if you have watched any small claims cases before your own trial date: the parties' versions of the facts are sometimes so different you can hardly believe they are talking about the same case.

Proving the elements of your claim

In Chapters 7, 8, and 9, you will see examples of what must be proved in a variety of types of cases. The things you have to prove are called **elements.** You must prove *all* of them in order to win your case. In a contract dispute, for example, the plaintiff must show the existence of a contract, the defendant breached the contract, the plaintiff tried to minimize losses as a result of the breach, and the plaintiff suffered damages as a result of the breach. The examples in Chapters 7, 8, and 9; your own research; or advice from a lawyer should have helped you determine the elements that you need to prove in order to prevail in your case. In this chapter, you will look at organizing your evidence in a way that a judge can easily understand. Your goal is to present your claim simply, clearly, and straightforwardly.

Looking at each element of your claim, ask yourself, "Who has knowledge about this element?" For example, consider this actual case: A builder sues a contractor for libel after he fired the contractor for doing shoddy work and falsifying bills. The contractor then knowingly writes false information about the plaintiff's reputation as a builder and circulates the information to some of the plaintiff's customers. The elements of a libel claim are:

- The defendant made statements in writing;
- The statements were false;
- The defendant knew they were false;
- The defendant circulated those statements among the builder's customers; and
- The plaintiff suffers financial harm as a result of the false statements (in this case, loses business)

How will the builder prove that the defendant made false statements in writing? One or more of his customers may have forwarded to the builder the contractor's defamatory e-mails to them, or mentioned the emails to the builder. The contractor might even have sent copies of his e-mails to the builder himself. The contractor may have threatened to ruin the builder's reputation with his customers, and the builder may have contacted some of his customers to see if they had received anything. To prove this element, the builder can

- Testify that he received copies of defamatory e-mails and the dates when he received them, and offer the e-mails into evidence.
- Subpoena one or more of his customers who can describe receiving defamatory e-mails, and who then can identify the e-mails.
- The builder can offer print-outs of the messages into evidence.

The builder probably does not have to do *all* of these things in order to prove this element; these are just some suggestions of what he might do.

How will the builder prove the statements were false and that the defendant knew they were false? The builder can testify that he received a telephone call from the contractor, who appeared to be very drunk, late on the Friday night following the firing. In that call, he will say, the defendant threatened to contact all his customers and try to ruin his reputation in retaliation for the builder's having fired the contractor. The builder should testify about his record with the Oregon Construction Contractors Board, which has received no complaints from any customers about his work in over 10 years. He may want to say how many homes he has built or remodeled during that time period to show how well-respected his work is.

The trail of defamatory e-mails will show that the defendant circulated the false information, and the builder has already offered those into evidence. The builder will need to testify that all the recipients are either current or former customers.

Finally, the builder must be able to show that he lost business as a result of the libel. If a potential customer was considering a bid from the builder for an $8,000 remodel of his guest house and then told the builder he would not consider him any more because of what he had heard about him from the contractor, the builder can testify that he lost business worth $8,000. Eight thousand dollars would be the amount of damages he seeks. He might want to subpoena the potential customer who decided not to hire him, so that the customer could describe his own reaction to the e-mail from the contractor. If any customers told others about the e-mails, their testimony may be helpful, too, to show that the builder may have future losses as a result of this false information. Since judges can decide to award less than the amount a claimant is asking for, this testimony would help convince the judge that the full amount requested would be fair.

In this example, the plaintiff uses his own testimony, documents (e-mails), and possibly the testimony of a witness to prove his case. You should do the same kind of analysis with your own case.

Preparing your case

A good first step in preparing for trial is to make a written outline of your claim (or counterclaim), element by element. Then write down what you will say or what other evidence you will offer to prove that element. Dates are often important in small claims cases. Make a timeline of your claim, showing each contact with the defendant or others who might be witnesses in some way to the dispute.

Find a couple of friends who will listen critically to you "present" your case. When you have presented it, see if they can explain your case to you. If they can, you know your presentation was clear. Ask them what else they might want to know about your case. Ask them for suggestions about other ways you might tell your story so that is simpler or clearer. Ask them what they might say if they were on the other side of the case to try to keep you from winning. Encourage them to stop you from dramatizing or saying things that seem to them like an exaggeration or a distortion of the facts. Exaggerations and distortions can look like lies to the judge.

The defendant's point of view

If you are the defendant in a small claims case, you, too, will need to think about the elements of the plaintiff's case. If, in the libel case described above, the plaintiff doesn't testify in court about an element of the claim or provide other proof about that element, the defendant can say to the judge, "Your Honor, plaintiff claims I libeled him, but damages are part of this kind of claim and he hasn't proved that he suffered any financial harm at all." Whether you would always want to do this is another matter. The judge could easily turn to the plaintiff and ask, "Well, do you have any damages as a result of defendant's written statements about you?" And the plaintiff could say, "Yes, your honor. Here are my sales documents from the following month..." Pay attention to what the plaintiff has or hasn't proved, and use your judgment about pointing out any deficiencies.

As the defendant, you will be listening to hear if the plaintiff leaves out any important facts or slants the facts in a way that helps her or him and hurts you. You will want to correct any misstated facts that are important. Again, dates can sometimes be critical; have your own calendar of contacts and activities.

Witnesses

Many small claims cases are of the "he said-she said" variety, where a judge listens to testimony of the parties only. There is no other evidence for the court to consider. The judge must decide, based on what the parties say, whom to believe. In other cases, the parties offer documents or things into evidence. In a few cases, one or more of the parties must rely on testimony of witnesses to help them make their case.

When do you need a witness? Whether you are the plaintiff or the defendant with a counterclaim, how you prove the elements of your claim will depend on who knows what. If you didn't see the teen-ager from down the street "key" your car but your neighbor did, your neighbor will be an essential witness when you sue the teen-ager and his parents for the damage to your car.

You don't get to choose who saw a car collision or who heard the used-car salesman tell you the car you were buying had just had brake work done and was perfectly safe to drive. But if more than one person can provide the same information that is important to your case, you don't need them all. The judge needs to hear the information only once. So think about the impression that each person is likely to make on the judge, and choose the one who can explain—clearly and believably—what happened.

A person who witnessed an event or activity may not support your side of the case. Before asking anyone to serve as a witness, ask the person at length about what he or she saw or heard or knows about your case. Take notes. If the person's recollection of important information differs from yours, you probably do not want this person to testify. You may end up seeing this person in court anyway, testifying for the other side in your case. If the person says something different in the courtroom than what that person said to you, and you took notes, you will be able to ask about the discrepancy. If you point out the discrepancy, the judge may tend to think the witness is not to be trusted.

Don't call a witness whose only connection to the case is that you asked him or her to show up; it's a waste of everyone's time. The judge is not going to listen to someone talk about what an honest and kindly person you are. If the witness doesn't have specific information about the case the judge has to decide, leave the witness out of the case.

Subpoenaing witnesses

A subpoena requires a person to show up in court. A subpoena is a type of court order. Not to comply is punishable as contempt of court.

Why would you need to subpoena a witness? Occasionally, a witness who promises to appear in person doesn't show up or isn't available by phone as promised—and you are left without information important to your case. It may do you no good to tell the judge, "My witness, who is the only one who saw the plaintiff tear up the contract, couldn't be here." Many judges will not allow you to testify about something that only someone else saw or heard. To prevent this problem, don't rely on a witness's promise; if you are not completely confident that the witness will follow through, subpoena the witness, even for a telephone appearance.

It's no surprise that many people do not want to testify. They don't like the idea of confrontation; they are afraid of going to court; they don't want to take time out of their busy day; they work and "can't" take time off; they may not like the person who needs their help in court; they may even have an outstanding arrest warrant and are worried they will be arrested if they appear. (They won't be.) In addition, the law doesn't allow some people to testify even if they want to unless they are subpoenaed—public officials, police, and other government workers, for example.

Sometimes people say they are willing to testify by telephone. Courts will sometimes grant permission for phone testimony when a party asks as far in advance as possible. If you don't get advance permission, it will usually be too late to ask for it at your hearing. Don't take that chance.

Whether it's a good idea to have a witness testify by telephone depends on why you need the witness. If the witness saw the driver who rear-ended your car, for example, and the defendant denies having been the driver, you want the witness to verify that the person she saw is the defendant in your case. She can't do that by phone. Likewise, if a witness has to review photographs or documents or identify items or explain diagrams or examine billing or medical records, etc., that you want to offer as evidence, the witness must appear in person. This logic applies to both ordinary witnesses and expert witnesses. (Expert witnesses are explained below.)

How to subpoena a witness

You can obtain blank subpoena forms from the court clerk. For each witness, you will need to deliver the subpoena yourself or have any adult deliver it. After the witness receives the subpoena, you file a proof of service form with the court. The court clerk can give you this form.

If your witnesses are all private citizens, there is no minimum time to deliver notices to them. It's courteous to deliver the subpoena as early as possible, of course, so that people can make plans to attend. If any witness is a public employee, early service is important. The witness will need enough time to notify his or her supervisor, and, in some cases, an agency lawyer before testifying.

Every witness is entitled to an appearance fee of $30 per day, plus 25 cents per mile of travel to and from the courthouse. If a subpoena is served without payment, the witness does not have to attend. You can't get a fee waiver or deferral in order to subpoena witnesses.

Do you need an expert?

In some cases, you may decide that you need an **expert witness.** An expert witness is someone who testifies about a technical aspect of evidence to help the judge understand facts that are important to your claim--such as the reactions of fabrics to certain chemicals during dry cleaning, the correct diagnosis of a car problem, what building standards apply to home improvements and the quality of specific improvements, the likely speed of a car based on the length of skid marks on the road, etc. An expert witness testifies on the basis of his or her advanced training, education, skill, or experience. Unlike an ordinary witness, the expert does not have to personally witness facts and events on which a case is based.

If you decide you need an expert, ask your proposed expert how he or she would explain the problem in your case to the judge. If what the expert says isn't crystal clear to someone who isn't an expert, you will need either to help the person speak in plain English or find another expert who can. Also be aware that a person who is an expert in one field may not qualify as an expert in another one. For example, the police officer who can testify as an expert about the speed of a car based on skid marks at the scene of an accident usually doesn't have the necessary background to testify about whether the road is properly banked at a corner. A civil engineer involved in highway construction would have to analyze that situation.

A witness who qualifies as an expert is often particularly unwilling to testify, because the testimony can cause long-term damage to relationships among professionals—doctors, dentists, lawyers, auto mechanics, building contractors all rely on others in their profession for referrals. Experts also may have to give up substantial income just to show up in court, and they have the right to charge the party who subpoenaed them for what amounts to their professional services.

If you win your case, you do not have the right to add the cost of an expert witness to your court costs. The other party will not have to reimburse you for this expense.

Ordinary witness or expert?

A single individual can sometimes be a general witness and sometimes an expert witness, or both in the same case. For example, after a traffic accident, a party might subpoena the officer at the scene to describe what he saw, or why he arrested the other party. In that situation, the officer is an ordinary witness because he is describing what he saw (heard, smelled, etc.) personally. If the party wants the officer to testify about the likely speed of the other car based on skid marks on the highway, the officer is acting as an expert witness because he has specialized knowledge about speed and distance evidence. He could make this analysis without having been at the scene. In a dispute over the need to repair a supposedly cracked Chevy head, another car mechanic can inspect the head and testify that there is no crack. In that case, the second mechanic may be testifying as an expert, even though he is basing his testimony on what he has personally observed. When the dispute is about whether the original mechanic is entitled to payment for work that was improperly performed, another mechanic could inspect the car and the work done on it, and then explain to the judge how the problem should have been handled to get the result that the customer paid for. In that situation, the second mechanic also would be testifying as an expert.

To rein in the cost of having an expert testify, ask the court clerk before your hearing date if you can have your case scheduled first or last so that the expert's time waiting in the courtroom is minimized. If your case is scheduled for the end of the court session, the court clerk may be able to give you a rough estimate of what time your case will start. With that information, you can alert the expert beforehand about when to appear.

Subpoenaing police

If one of your witnesses is a police officer, the subpoena process is a little more complicated. The subpoena must be delivered at least 10 days before the hearing date. The subpoena should go to the officer personally, the officer's supervisor, or to the person at the officer's agency who is designated to accept subpoenas. Before sending someone to the agency with the subpoena, call ahead a few days to make sure that at least one of those people will be available on the day the subpoena is to be served.

If the police officer is a witness to one or more facts in the case—what he or she observed at the scene, whether the other party was arrested, etc.—the usual fee rules apply. If you are calling on the police officer to testify as an expert, the subpoena must say on its face that the officer is being called as an expert witness. The subpoena must be accompanied by a payment of $160. This amount is an estimate of what the agency will be paying in salary to an officer who is doing your business instead of agency business. The actual cost may be different. If it is less, the agency will refund the unused amount, usually within a month. If the cost is higher, you may be billed for the difference. You are responsible for paying the difference only if the agency sends its bill within seven days after the officer's court appearance.

Police Reports

You may want or need to use a police report to support your side of a case. For example, you may be suing your landlord for breaching your right as a tenant to "quiet enjoyment" of your home after you've had to call the police a dozen times about midnight rowdiness or violence of other tenants and the landlord has refused to intervene. Police reports will help you document the number of times you called for help. After a traffic accident, a police report can help you in several ways—finding out which police officers came to the scene, whether they took pictures or drew a diagram of the accident, whether the opposing party was cited for having caused the wreck or arrested for drunk driving, etc. Sometimes the opposing party will even have acknowledged blame to the police. The report may contain witness names and contact information, too.

There are different types of reports:

- Police narrative reports (including incident reports and arrest reports)
- Traffic crash/exchange of information reports
- Citations (tickets) themselves
- Arrest summaries (criminal history reports)

Getting a copy of a police report of an incident that affected you should be easy—but it's not. First, each Oregon county has its own system for finding and issuing reports. You'll need to talk to the individual police agency for specific instructions on its system. Second, if you don't have specific information such as names and dates, the police may not even be able to find the records you are seeking. (Not being able to find records is more likely when the police wrote an "incident report," after responding but not arresting anyone.)

Finding a report can take time, especially now that funding for police staffing has been cut. One county asks for up to seven working days; in another, staff say it can take as long as three weeks to get the requested information. If you think you will need a report, ask for it as soon as you can. Getting copies of reports will cost you--fees vary from county to county, but expect to pay a minimum of $10. You can't get this fee waived by the court.

Here's the kind of information you will need to provide in order to get a report:

- Your name, phone number, email address, your company or organization if you're asking on its behalf
- The type of incident and the reason you want the information ("as evidence in small claims court case"), dates, locations, names and other contact information.

Preparing witnesses (and yourself!) to testify

The most important thing that witnesses—including you—must do is tell the truth about what you know about the case. The second most important thing is for witnesses to get to the point. They can do that most easily if you take the time to explain to them the legal points that you must make in your case, and the facts they need to talk about to help you make those points.

Your ordinary witnesses should testify about what they know personally because of something they saw or heard. They should stick to the facts, not raising their opinions or conclusions. They should be familiar with all relevant dates and times, and should be able to justify how they know those dates and times so they can explain why to the judge if they are asked.

You and your witnesses are allowed to practice what you are going to say in court, so long as everything is truthful. And you should practice! Write down your questions for your witnesses, making a note if you have some item of evidence they need to look at as they testify. Then, practice asking them the questions that you plan to ask in court and practice handing them each item of evidence and asking them to identify it. Have your witnesses write down what they are going to say, and ask them to practice saying it several times before trial. (Witnesses should not bring these statements to court because they will be tempted to read them rather than testify from memory. A witness who reads looks much less truthful; and some judges forbid the witnesses, and you, from reading.)Your questions to your witnesses should be as simple as possible.

For example, for a witness who was at the scene of a car accident, you might say, "Were you present at the corner of Seventh Street and G Street in Grants Pass at around 2 p.m. on March 12 of this year?" The witness will answer, "Yes." Your next question will be "What did you see?" The witness will then describe the accident, including whether the other party appeared to be at fault because of running a red light, talking on a cell phone, driving too fast for conditions, etc. You will need the witness to identify the other driver, too, as the defendant. If you have created a chart, you can ask the witness to show where she was standing when she saw the accident, and to show where the cars were before and at the time of impact.

Parties in small claims court usually don't cross-examine each other or the other party's witnesses, and some judges don't allow it, but make your witnesses aware that the other side may have questions for them. How should they respond to those questions? They should listen to the question, make sure they understand the question, and, if they do, answer the question. If they don't have the information the other side wants to know, their answer to the question should be, "I don't know." We are always tempted to guess—but telling "the truth, the whole truth, and nothing but the truth" doesn't allow for guessing.

Let your witnesses know that they may have to wait outside the courtroom until it is their turn to testify. Depending on how many cases are ahead of yours, they may be waiting there for two to three hours. They should bring with them any medications they need, and, if they have children, should be sure to let the caregiver know that it could be a long morning or afternoon.

There's one more aspect to preparing your witnesses to testify. How they look and how they act in court will affect the judge's perception of you and your case. Like you, they should dress conservatively, talk respectfully, and refrain from reacting to what occurs by making faces or remarks.

What about "hearsay"?

Sometimes people think they aren't allowed to say things in court that are "hearsay." Don't worry about it! There are some 30 exceptions to the "hearsay rule." Furthermore, small claims court does not have to follow the strict rules of evidence. So don't assume that you can't say something you want to say because it's "just hearsay." Say what you need to say. The judge will let you know if there's a problem with it.

Preparing your exhibits

If you have photos or documents that you will be offering as evidence at trial, make copies of all of them—one set for the judge, one set for yourself, and one set for the other party. If there is nothing on the backs of the documents, number them on the back in case you need to refer to more than one of them at a time at your hearing. Many people do not make copies for themselves or the other side, and waste a lot of time walking back and forth between the judge's bench and counsel tables to show each item. Don't put marks on the front of any document or photo that goes to the judge or the other party. You are free to make marks on your own copies. As you develop your case, think about when you should offer your documents so they are most helpful to telling your story.

Once the judge accepts things as evidence, the judge can then take them into account when making a decision. If the judge does not admit something into evidence, the judge cannot consider it when making a decision.

"Drawing a picture"

In some kinds of cases, one of the best tools for showing the judge how something happened is a chart or a diagram. Suppose, for example, you are in court to get damages from a landlord whose rental became a drug house and who did nothing about it for months. You may want to make a list of dates you were unable to sleep because of raucous behavior next door, the number of times you called the police, the number of times the police came when you didn't call them, the times you had to pick up syringes or other drug gear off the street or from your own yard, days when the drug dealers next door threatened you, the times you contacted the landlord to complain. Or your case may have come about as the result of a fender bender. A diagram of the streets, with street names and an indicator of north/south and east/west, may help the judge understand what happened. If the other party objects to a diagram because it's not "to scale," you can agree that it is not—your only goal is to give the judge a better idea of what the dispute is about. Diagrams and charts like these are not evidence in themselves, so you won't offer them as exhibits.

Any diagram or chart should have printing that is large enough to be seen from a distance, or the judge will miss the point you are trying to make. Be sure to have a way to display the chart, too. Many courtrooms have easels where you can display posters. Ask the court clerk if one can be made available for your use; check with the judge's trial assistant on the day before or the day of trial to ensure that you can get access to it—or bring your own stand for it.

A final note: Don't use this tool just because it's there. Use it only if it's going to be helpful to the judge's understanding of the case.

Using technology

It's becoming more common for people to offer video footage, cell phone messages, and other "high tech" information as evidence in their cases. But many people don't realize that they must provide a way to view or hear their information, too. If you plan to use electronic media in your case, make sure you have the technology to make it accessible to the judge. A judge is not likely to take time out in the middle of your hearing to log on to a relevant Web site or read a CD. Print out copies of documents that are important to your case!

Caution: A few courthouses have security rules against bringing cell phones or other media equipment into the building. This prohibition can sometimes create a problem. For example, if the opposing party in your case left you a cell phone message that is important evidence, contact the court clerk's office in advance to find out if cell phones are prohibited. If they are, find out how you can get permission to bring yours in for use in the case. Or talk to a "techie" about a different way to bring the voice message or other electronic data into the courtroom. Don't put off doing these things until the week of trial.

Friends and family in the courtroom

If you have young children or children who have trouble behaving, find child care for them while you are in court. Children can be a distraction for you and for the judge who is trying to resolve your legal problem.

As for friends and adult family members, it's always nice to have someone nearby for moral support. But you have to warn these people that they, too, can have a negative effect on your case if they are disruptive. All the people who are associated with you should be on their best behavior.

CHAPTER 7

Making your case, part 1: Common claims and defenses

Before you file a claim or a counterclaim in small claims court, you need to know whether you "have a case": is there law to support your position? Different situations are covered by different laws. This chapter gives you an overview of two general categories of cases, and then looks at *just a few* of the typical situations that land people in small claims court. Chapters 8 and 9 examine a few other typical problems. Together, they lay out what the plaintiff needs to prove in those cases in order to win, and what the defendant needs to prove in order to keep the plaintiff from winning.

How strong does your case have to be?

Whether you are the plaintiff or a defendant with a counterclaim, you have to "prove" your case. You may have heard that the prosecution must prove its case "beyond a reasonable doubt." That's true in a criminal case—but not in civil cases such as those in small claims court. Here, you must prove your case by only a "preponderance of the evidence." What does that mean? It means that, once the judge has heard all the facts, he or she will conclude that your version of what happened is *more likely than not* what happened. It also means that you have given evidence of all the things you need to show (the **elements** of your claim) in order to win your case.

The two main categories of cases

Most small claims fall into two large categories—contracts and torts. These categories come with different elements for the plaintiff or counter claimant to prove. Let's look at contracts first. A contract is an agreement, written or oral, that is enforceable. Parties to a contract each agree to do something of value in exchange for something else of value. **Some examples of enforceable contracts:**

- A residential landlord offers safe, decent housing to a tenant in exchange for rent and careful use of the home.
- A car dealer offers cars and trucks in exchange for cash.
- An employer agrees to pay employees a certain wage for the work they do.
- My friend Nancy offers a reward to the person who finds and returns her beloved labradoodle.
- You lend me money (by personal loan, by issuing me a credit card, or letting me have a mortgage) in exchange for my paying the money back with interest.

Not all agreements are contracts. If Tony promises his daughter Meadow that he will give her $10,000 at Christmas and then changes his mind, can Meadow sue him successfully? No. Meadow hasn't promised to do anything to be entitled to the money, so Tony's promise isn't enforceable. If Tony promises Meadow $10,000 to become a criminal defense attorney and she goes to law school, passes the New Jersey bar examination, and gets a job in the public defender's office, she can take Tony to small claims court if he refuses to pay—because she's done something he required in exchange for his promise to pay. Another example: If Ira and I agree to meet this evening for a poker game at the Lotus Club in Portland, we've made an agreement—but we haven't made a contract. We haven't agreed to do or give something of value in exchange for something else of value.

When a contract is enforceable, someone who doesn't or isn't able to do what is promised is said to have **breached** the contract. People who owe money under a contract but don't or can't pay it as agreed make up a large percentage of defendants in small claims cases.

While contracts can be enforced if they are oral rather than written, there are some limitations on which oral contracts can be enforced. Oral contracts cannot be enforced if they

- Involve a real estate sale or purchase;
- Involve more than $500 of goods or property; or
- Can't be performed within a year. (Example: a ten-year lease must be in writing to be enforceable, because performing the duties under the lease will take more than one year. A kitchen remodeling job can theoretically be completed within a year, however, even if it actually takes longer.)

That's why businesses always want a written contract when they sell goods on anything other than a "walk in and pay cash" basis. Still, it doesn't take much for a contract to qualify as written. Courts have found that a contract is valid and enforceable under the rule above even if the only evidence is as limited as an email message that lets the other party know when a shipment for that party is due to arrive.

Rights and duties under many contracts are pretty simple. Some can be more complex. For example, if one party refuses to perform its duties under a contract because it learns information that makes it think the other party can't pay for the work, has the first party breached the contract? The answer is: "That depends." Other contracts may be subject to state or federal legal requirements that create a duty or a right. For example, most employees are entitled to two 10-minute breaks per eight-hour work shift, even if an employer never mentions that right to workers. Most employees are entitled to receive a minimum wage, and workers' compensation benefits for on-the-job injuries, even if the employer never says so. While landlords and tenants of commercial properties (stores, factories, offices, etc.) are generally free to contract for rights and duties as they wish, residential landlords have obligations under state law that they cannot violate, regardless of what the rental agreement says. Those in the business of manufacturing products for personal, family, or household use have a legal duty to make the product safe for intended and other foreseeable uses.

A few contracts are subject to "cooling off" rules under federal or state laws. These laws allow people who have agreed to buy consumer products or services to cancel their contract to purchase these things once they've had time to think over what they have signed. Depending on the product or service, the time limits to back out of the contract vary. *Most contracts do NOT have a cooling-off period!*

Defining "tort" is a little harder. In very general terms, it is conduct that society finds unacceptable; sometimes the conduct is even a crime. Punching someone can be a tort (assault/battery); keeping something that someone lent to you can be a tort (conversion). From a neighbor's perspective, the operation of a drug house next door can be a tort (nuisance). Accidentally driving over the neighbor's prize rose bushes can be a tort (trespass and property damage).

As you can see, there's no contract involved in these examples. But sometimes a tort can also be a breach of a contract. You contract with a doctor to do work for you for a fee, for example. If a surgery or other service is sloppy and puts you in a worse position that you would have been without the service, you may have a tort claim against the doctor (malpractice). You contract with a car mechanic's shop for an oil change. It then forgets to add oil to your engine after the oil change, ruining your car's engine. That's a tort (negligence) as well as a breach of contract.

There's a common thread in all of these tort examples:

- Society expects people not to hurt others or the property of others, either on purpose or by being reckless or careless
- Some behavior violates this social standard
- Some behavior that violates the social standard causes harm to others

All claims involving torts will have to establish that there is a standard of acceptable behavior, that the defendant (or the plaintiff against whom the defendant has a counterclaim) carelessly or intentionally did something that he or she should know presents a risk of harm to others, and that the claimant actually suffered harm as a result of the other party's conduct. In a few cases, someone who *fails* to do something the person has a duty to do can be a tort, too.

Here's a real-life example of a tort claim for defamation (slander or libel). A builder sues for libel after a contractor knowingly writes false information about the plaintiff's reputation as a builder and circulates the information to some of the plaintiff's customers. **The plaintiff must show that:**

- The defendant made statements in writing (oral statements would be slander; it's the writing that makes them libel)
- The statements were false
- The defendant knew they were false or didn't have a reason to believe they were true
- The defendant circulated those statements among the builder's customers
- AND the builder lost business as a result of the false statements.

These are all elements of a claim for libel. If the plaintiff shows that the first four things occurred, but cannot show that he lost business as a result of the libel, he will not win his case. In addition, the plaintiff has sued for a certain amount of money that he or she claims as damages—the amount of business lost as a result of the libel. He must be able to explain to the judge how he came up with that estimate of his losses.

The vast majority of claims involve either tort or contract law. If your potential claim doesn't seem to fit one or both categories, some other kind of legal category may apply. Get legal advice or research your problem further before heading for court.

Typical contract claims and defenses

Below are samples of claims and defenses in residential landlord-tenant cases, followed by samples of claims and defenses in employee wage claims. In Chapters 8 and 9, you can see examples of other types of contract cases, including debt collection and consumer law claims, and tort cases.

RESIDENTIAL LANDLORD-TENANT

1. Landlord claim for damage to rental unit

The problem: When tenants moved out, they left discarded belongings and garbage, and destroyed landlord property in their wake.

What landlord must establish (the elements of the claim):

- Landlord and tenants had rental agreement
- Rental was in good condition when tenants moved in

- Rental was not in good condition when tenants moved out
- Specific repair problems that landlord had to address
- Cost to landlord (after using all of tenants' security deposit) of repairs to rental, including the reasonable amount of time the rental was off the market while repairs were made

Landlord's proof: photos (preferably from before tenants moved in and then after tenants moved out); copy of rental agreement; copy of move-in checklist and move-out checklist, if any; police reports, if any; testimony of landlord and of person or persons who helped clean and make repairs about what they did and how much time it took them, what materials and cleaning supplies they had to buy or rent in order to do the job

Tenants' possible defenses against damage claim:

- Rental was in same or similar condition on move-out as at move-in
- Tenants left rental in good condition, but others entered the unit after they moved out and damaged the rental
- Amount of claim too high for work done; claim is made in bad faith
- Landlord gave no itemized list of damage within 31 days of move- out and gave no notice of damage claim before filing small claim case
- Landlord waited more than a year to seek payment—too late to file suit

Tenants' proof: photos (preferably from time tenants moved in as well as when tenants moved out); copy of move-in checklist, if helpful, or letters or emails to landlord requesting repairs; testimony from tenants and others about what the rental looked like at move-in and move-out, what they did to clean and repair rental at move-out; that the landlord waited a period of time after tenants moved before conducting inspection, allowing or making it possible for others to enter the property; documentation of when tenants moved out (notices, letters, key receipt, final utility bills, etc)

2. Landlord claim for unpaid rent

The problem: Tenants are living in unit and owe back rent, or (more commonly) tenants moved out of unit owing rent

What landlord must establish:

- Existence of landlord-tenant relationship
- Amount of rent due under written or oral contract
- Due date of rent payments
- Amount of rent tenants did not pay by due date
- Late fees, if any, for nonpayment
- Total amount due as damages to landlord

Landlord's proof: written rental agreement, if any, showing rent amount, due date, and late fee amount, if any; testimony about payments not received and calculation of late fees, if any

Note: A claim for unpaid rent is not the same kind of case in which a residential landlord wants to evict tenants for nonpayment of rent. Eviction cases are filed in circuit court, not small claims court.

Tenants' possible defenses against rent claim:

- Landlord failed to make required repairs, reducing value of rental unit (over a period as long as the preceding 12 months) and was therefore not entitled to rent
- Landlord allowed nonpayment or accepted partial payments of rent, waiving right to full or timely payment or right to impose late fees
- Tenants' rent was garnished by third party collecting on a judgment against landlord
- Landlord's claim was filed more than one year after rent unpaid

Tenants' proof: photos, documents, showing requests for repairs, reduced value of rental, writ of garnishment forms; testimony of tenants, others, including reason for amount of reduction of rental value claimed or basis for waiver of right to rent payment timely or late fees. *Note: These can be fairly technical defenses, based on provisions of the Oregon Residential Landlord and Tenant Act. You should become very familiar with the language of the statute, as the success of your defense will depend on specific words in the law. Get legal advice if at all possible before attempting either of these defenses. See Appendix B.*

3. Tenants' claim for damages for lack of habitability of rental

The problem: Tenants are living in or were living in, over a period up to the last 12 months, a unit that substantially lacked the criteria for safe and decent housing under Oregon Residential Landlord and Tenant Act (ORLTA).

Tenants must establish:

- They were tenants under ORLTA
- Amount of rent due, amount of rent paid
- Conditions in rental did not meet habitability requirements of the law
- Tenants did not cause any of the habitability problems
- Landlord knew or should have known of problems
- Problems interfered with tenants' ability to get full benefit of rental
- Dollar amount by which value of rental reduced (damages)

Tenants' proof: photos, letters or emails to landlord, rent receipts or other proof of payment; testimony of tenants, building inspectors about inability to use unit fully or safely, calculations of amount of reduction in value of rental

Landlord's possible defenses against habitability claims:

- Tenants were not residential tenants covered by ORLTA
- Tenants had not paid rent
- Landlord had no notice of habitability problems
- Minor problem was made much worse because tenants did not report the problem in a timely manner or take other steps to keep problem from worsening
- Tenants had caused habitability problems
- Tenants had refused to let landlord or landlord's workers onto premises to fix habitability problems
- Tenants waited more than one year to file some or all of their claims

Landlord's proof: photos, non-residential rental agreement or land sale contract agreement, emails to and from workers, bills from workers, rent receipts; testimony of landlord, workers, others with knowledge of condition of rental

4. Tenants' claim for damages caused by residential landlord's lockout or utility or services shutoff or reduction

The problem: Residential landlord changed locks in rental, shut off water or other utilities such as heat and electricity, or made it impossible for tenants to use other services included in rental agreement

Tenants must establish:

- Tenants are protected by ORLTA
- Tenants lived in unit belonging to landlord within the last 12 months
- Landlord turned off services or locked tenants out of rental at some time during that 12-month period without first lawfully terminating the tenancy by giving proper notice and obtaining a court judgment of eviction
- Tenants' actual damages (such as rotted food resulting from lack of electricity, the need to stay in a motel, etc.) if they are larger than statutory damages; otherwise, assertion of right to statutory damages

Tenants' proof: tenants' testimony; copy of rental agreement and any correspondence with landlord about shutoff or reduction in services; testimony of utility company employee or other provider, or locksmith, etc.

Landlord's possible defenses:

- Tenants were not residential tenants covered by ORLTA
- Landlord reasonably believed tenants had abandoned premises
- Claim arose more than one year prior to filing and is therefore too late

Landlord's proof: landlord's testimony; copy of rental agreement

5. Tenants' claim for statutory damages caused by landlord's retaliatory conduct against tenants for exercising their right to habitable housing

The problem: Tenants asked landlord to make repairs to rental; landlord responded with 60-day "no cause" notice of eviction or other conduct whose purpose or effect seemed retaliatory.

Tenants must establish:

- They are residential tenants of landlord, protected by ORLTA
- They asked landlord to repair a habitability problem at rental within last 12 months
- Tenants did not cause the habitability problem themselves, either negligently or intentionally
- Landlord retaliated against them for seeking repairs
- Tenants are entitled to statutory damages

Tenants' proof: tenants' testimony, testimony of anyone who warned them of landlord's history of retaliation; rental agreement, dated notice to landlord asking for repairs, any documents showing landlord's retaliation

Landlord's possible defenses:

- Landlord never received tenants' request for repairs, therefore response could not have been retaliatory
- Tenants are not residential tenants
- Landlord had good, non-retaliatory reason for conduct
- Tenants were behind in rent, therefore could not make a claim of retaliation

Landlord's proof: testimony; copies of rental agreement, payment history

Claims for retaliation can be difficult for tenants to prove. While ORLTA used to presume retaliation was the reason a landlord attempted to raise rent, terminate rental agreement, etc. following tenants' requests for repairs, the presumption was removed from the law some years ago—even though the termination notice or rent hike is almost invariably retaliatory. Tenants rarely have proof in the form of a nasty letter or phone message from their landlord in order to meet this requirement. Get some guidance about the status of the law before filing a retaliation case.

Can the landlord win by alleging tenants can't claim retaliation if they are behind in their rent? Sometimes. The answer depends on how severe the habitability problem is and how long it has existed. Tenants who are "behind" on their rent may not in fact OWE any rent if the rental, because of

the habitability problem, is worth less than the landlord says is due. Tenants should always get legal advice before taking on this kind of case, as this claim can become fairly complex.

6. Tenants' claim for statutory damages for landlord's wrongful entry

The problem: Landlord or agent of landlord enters tenants' rental without advance notice and without permission, in non-emergency situation.

Tenants must establish:

- They are residential tenants protected by ORLTA.
- Landlord entered rental without advance notice and without permission in non-emergency situations
- Unlawful entry occurred within the last 12 months
- Tenants are entitled to statutory damages

Tenants' proof: their testimony and that of any witnesses to landlord entry, including dates and times; copy of rental agreement

Landlord's possible defenses:

- No entry was made
- Entry was made after proper notice
- Entry was made for purpose of repairs within seven days after a request from tenants for repairs or was a prompt continuation of requested work started within the seven-day period
- Entry was justified by emergency
- Landlord reasonably believed tenants had abandoned premises
- Tenants not residential tenants protected by ORLTA

Landlord's proof: testimony re notice given or lack of entry, request for repairs by tenants, existence of emergency, reasons landlord believed tenants had abandoned the premises; copy of non-residential rental agreement or other document explaining tenants' presence at unit

7. Tenants' claim for security deposit

The problem: (1) Tenants paid security deposit and didn't get it back when they moved, nor did they get explanation from landlord how deposit was used;

or (2) tenants believe landlord retained excessive amount of deposit for alleged repairs.

Tenants must establish:

- Tenants were residential tenants within the period of one year and 31 days before filing case
- Tenants paid security deposit
- Tenants left rental clean and in good condition on move-out
- Tenants did not timely receive security deposit or a portion of the deposit and/or a detailed statement of use of deposit to clean or repair rental; or statement alleged excessive amount for work performed

Tenants' proof: testimony about what they did to leave unit clean and in good condition, and what a reasonable charge for repairs or cleaning would be based on landlord's timely notice of keeping all or part of the deposit; receipt for security deposit, photos or video of unit at time of move-out, receipts for purchase of cleaning supplies, rental of steam cleaner, etc.

Landlord's possible defenses:

- Tenants were not residential tenants protected by ORLTA
- Landlord timely returned payment by mail even though tenants did not receive it
- Landlord had no mailing address for tenants and tenants did not have their mail forwarded, so timely notice went to their old address
- Landlord's claims for cleaning and repair were justified
- Tenants received and cashed returned deposit and are not entitled to any additional payment

Landlord's proof: testimony of landlord and persons involved in cleaning and repair; photos; receipts for materials and supplies; returned envelope containing payment or statement; copy of check.

UNPAID WAGES

The problem: An employee leaves the job—and then doesn't get compensated for the final work period.

Before filing in small claims court for your back wages or commissions, you should report the problem to the Oregon Bureau of Labor and Industries. In a few cases, that agency may take the case on your behalf. It also may be able to help you if your former employer has been taken over by a court receiver. If small claims court is the route you must take, however,

Plaintiff who was not paid all wages must establish:

- Plaintiff was employee of employer
- Date of employment and last date
- Wages or salary and commission schedule
- Normal payday
- Amount unpaid when job ended
- Amount of penalty to which plaintiff is entitled (see below)

Plaintiff's proof: testimony; copies of timesheets, regular pay stubs, other evidence of times and days worked and amount of pay, written demand for payment.

Employer's possible defenses:

- Employer paid all wages due
- Employee's calculations of dates, amount worked are wrong
- Employer is financially unable to pay wages and is therefore not subject to penalty
- Written authorization by employee for employer to deduct up to 25 per cent of final pay for repayment of cash loan to employee documented in writing and in employer's records

Refusing to pay employee because employee allegedly stole from the business or was lazy, etc., is not a legal defense for not having paid wages.

Employer's proof: testimony; payroll records; financial records of business

Oregon law provides for a penalty against former employers who do not pay wages and commissions when they are financially able to pay. The penalty is either:

- An additional amount of wages, equal to eight hours per day for up to

30 days or until a lawsuit is filed, whichever comes first, if the plaintiff has sent written noticed demanding payment before filing the claim and employer does not pay within 12 days of receiving the demand; or

- Up to 100 per cent of the amount of unpaid wages if the plaintiff has not sent a written demand for payment or if the employer paid the wages due within 12 days of receiving notice.

Thus, if you made a written demand for payment and the employer did not pay in response, one of the things you must prove is that you made a written demand for payment if you want to maximize the penalty you can claim.

UNLAWFUL DEDUCTIONS FROM EMPLOYEE PAY

Problem: Employer withholds money from employee's pay that the employee hasn't authorized and that the law doesn't require the employer to withhold.

Plaintiff employee must establish:

- Rate of pay, after deductions for payroll taxes, Medicare, Social Security (and union dues, if a union member), and lawful garnishments
- Employer has withheld additional amounts
- Employee has not agreed to having additional amounts withheld, or
- If employee did agree to having additional amounts withheld, those funds were not withheld to benefit the employee and are therefore unlawful
- Damages (the larger of $200 or the amount unlawfully withheld)

Plaintiff's proof: testimony; pay stubs, other documents relating to wages

Defendant employer's possible defenses:

- All deductions were legally required
- Any deduction not required by law was by written authorization of employee and for employee's benefit and recorded in payroll records

Defendant's proof: testimony; employee's authorization, business financial records

FAILURE TO PAY OVERTIME

The problem: Employer subject to overtime laws fails to pay employee overtime pay

Plaintiff who was not paid overtime wages must establish:

- Plaintiff was employee of employer during period within two years of filing claim
- Dates of employment and last date
- Employer was subject to overtime pay laws
- Wages or salary and commission schedule
- Number of overtime hours worked, and when worked
- Amount unpaid

Plaintiff's proof: testimony; copies of timesheets, regular pay stubs, other evidence of times and days worked and amount of pay

Employer's possible defenses:

- Employer paid all wages due
- Employee's calculations of dates, amount worked are wrong
- Employee working overtime did so without knowledge or consent of employer and in direct violation of instructions not to work overtime
- Employer not subject to Oregon overtime law
- Employer subject to different overtime laws than law plaintiff relies on
- The plaintiff waited too long to file claim

Employer's proof: employer's testimony, testimony of others familiar with business policy regarding overtime and hours plaintiff worked; personnel and payroll records, other documents relating to hours worked, lack of authorization to work overtime hours

For other common examples of contract claims in small claims court, see Chapter 8. For common examples of tort cases, see Chapter 9.

CHAPTER 8

Making your case, part 2: Typical contract problems

Chapter 7 introduced you to basic elements of contract and tort claims, and gave you some examples of typical kinds of claims that end up in small claims court, such as those based on residential landlord-tenant disputes and wage claims. It also described some situations in which a breach of contract could also be a tort.

This chapter looks at more cases involving typical contract problems.

There are two general categories of contract cases that can take place in small claims court: those based on general business transactions and those based on consumer transactions. Consumer cases involve purchases of things or services from commercial sellers for personal, family, or household use. They include debts arising from installment contracts for home appliances and furniture, personal credit card purchases, payments to local businesses for personal or home products or services, and much more. The difference matters because consumers have some defenses against creditors that are different from those in non-consumer cases.

Likewise, a non-consumer contract is more likely to have provisions for damages that are specific to that contract. For example, some contracts allow for **liquidated damages**—an amount of money that the parties think will approximate what a breach of contract might cost one side or the other. Some contracts may require the parties to **arbitrate** their dispute; small claims court might not even be an option. If there's a written contract, read it and make sure you understand what you are allowed or required to do--before you sue.

General elements in breach-of-contract cases

UNPAID DEBT—NON-CONSUMER

The problem: The most common breach-of-contract claim is that someone got a product or service without paying for it or without paying for it in full.

The plaintiff creditor must establish:

- The debt exists
- Payment is due
- The defendant hasn't paid it

Plaintiff's proof: testimony of existence of contract, effective date, and purpose, that plaintiff fulfilled his or her part of the agreement, when payment was due, how much is owed; copy of contract, record of payments made (if any)

The defendant debtor's possible defenses

- Creditor breached contract first—creditor's work or product was seriously defective or substandard, creditor delayed providing work or products beyond any reasonable time, etc., causing debtor to lose money
- Creditor and debtor changed terms of contract after creditor agreed to provide product or do work so that debtor is not in breach
- Creditor obtained debtor's agreement to contract by fraud
- Debtor made all payments under the contract
- Debtor had to have substandard product repaired or substandard work redone by another at debtor's expense, and those amounts should be deducted from the contract fee
- Contract provided for "liquidated damages" (a set dollar amount) and creditor cannot ask for more than that amount
- Creditor has waited too long to file the case

Defendant debtor's proof: testimony about creditor's breach; copy of contract, any later documents showing change in terms; record of payments made to creditor or to others to fix defects in creditor's work or products.

BOUNCED CHECKS

The problem: Merchant accepts a check that is dishonored by the bank. The merchant not only doesn't get paid for a good or service; it also must pay the bank a dishonored check fee.

Merchant must establish:

- Check was written by defendant
- Defendant either lacked funds in account or stopped payment on check
- To qualify for statutory damages of three times the amount of the dishonored check, merchant made a written demand to defendant for payment more than 30 days before filing claim, and defendant did not pay

Plaintiff's proof: testimony; dishonored check in defendant's name, copy of demand letter if seeking triple statutory damages

Check user's possible defenses:

- Check written by another without knowledge or consent of defendant (fraud, forgery, or identity theft)
- Good cause to stop payment on check

Defendant's proof: testimony of defendant about good cause; testimony of police, handwriting expert; police reports

Being unaware that the check wasn't good or adding money to the account too late for the check to clear is NOT a legal defense in this kind of case.

CONSUMER DEBT

The problem: Someone who buys or rents a product or a service for family, personal, or household use (including medical and dental care) does not pay for it. The elements of the creditor's case are the same as above, but the consumer's defenses are sometimes different:

- There is no debt, because creditor is suing the wrong person
- Creditor is suing for the wrong amount
- Consumer has paid off the debt
- Product was defective and was returned to seller
- Creditor has waited too long to file the case
- Creditor can't prove it has the right to collect the debt (because, for example, the debt has passed through many hands and documentation has been lost. It's the creditor's job to maintain all records. It has no right to sue if it cannot show it is the real party in interest.)
- Product was so defective it could not be used for its intended purpose, consumer notified seller of the problem, and creditor refused to correct the defect
- Product was under warranty that seller refused to honor when product broke or failed to perform
- Consumer and creditor entered into different payment agreement than that in original contract, consumer abided fully by the new agreement, and creditor did not honor new agreement
- Consumer exercised right under "cooling off" statutes to cancel contract and creditor refused to return consumer's money (applies to most door-to-door and unsolicited phone sales; some time shares and campground memberships; health club memberships; hearing aids, power wheelchairs, and other assistive devices)
- Efforts to collect the debt, even if the debt itself is valid, violated state or federal law (see Appendix B for more information; there is a long list of collection abuses that can give rise to statutory damages for the wronged consumer)

Defendant's proof: testimony about transaction and action taken after transaction, witness testimony about defects or repairs needed; contract, warranties, and any other proof of communication or agreement of the parties; proof of mailing of notices and documents; receipts for repairs made

Note about medical bills: Sometimes people who are dissatisfied with the outcome of medical treatment decide not to pay for the service, and try to use this reason as a defense to a collection case against them. It won't work. You must counterclaim for damages for medical malpractice, or bring a separate case against the provider. See the tort section in Chapter 9 for information about what you must prove in order to win a malpractice case.

For certain problems, Oregon law provides some very specific remedies that you likely won't know about. For example, the legislature acted to protect purchasers of puppies and dogs from "puppy mills" by requiring retail pet stores to provide a history of the animal, information about registration, typical health conditions suffered by certain breeds, and other information, all in writing. A retailer can be forced to take back a diseased or deformed dog under some circumstances, provide a replacement dog, or pay for veterinary bills associated with a health problem the retailer didn't disclose to the buyer. Another example is a law that forces car dealers to give back a buyer's trade-in if the seller can't find financing for the buyer on exactly the same terms the parties agreed to originally. This law came about because dishonest dealers would unload trade-ins before the deal was complete, forcing the purchaser to accept a new deal worse for the customer than the original one. The purchaser has the right to sue for the return of the old car or the value of the old car along with the right to reject the new deal.

These examples show how important it is to research your case before you file it: your remedies may be limited in some types of cases, or you may have remedies beyond what you might expect. Do your homework. Then get legal advice. Below are some more common examples of cases in which the plaintiff can or must take additional steps before filing a lawsuit.

HOME CONSTRUCTION AND IMPROVEMENTS

One very common area of problems is home construction and improvements. In the typical case, a homeowner hires a builder or handy person to build a house, add a garage or deck, repair or replace a leaky roof, install plumbing for a second bathroom or wiring in the basement, or fix that creaky old staircase. When the contractor finishes the job, the homeowner may refuse to pay for the work—usually because the homeowner is dissatisfied with the job.

Options for the homeowner

The "price tag" in some of these cases is too high for small claims court. For example, in the last couple of years, some homeowners have learned that the dry wall used in the construction of their homes contained toxic chemicals.

Removal and replacement may involve several defendants (not only the builder but also the manufacturing company). In other cases, construction materials have contributed to the growth of toxic mold. These cases may require the use of expert witnesses and extensive testing. For advice about what you might be up against, find a lawyer who handles construction cases.

In cases involving remodels and repairs to an existing home, small claims court is often a good option. If the contractor is not licensed and bonded by the state, the homeowner can go directly to small claims court. Under Oregon law, a contractor who is not licensed and bonded by the state cannot raise any claims against a homeowner. With the right proof, the plaintiff homeowner can win a case against an unregistered builder—and the builder cannot counterclaim. Getting payment from an unlicensed and unbonded contractor can be difficult, however.

If the contractor is licensed and bonded by the state, the homeowner must take other steps first. The first step is to send a "notice of defect" to the contractor, by registered mail, return receipt requested. The notice must go to the last known address for the contractor listed in the records of the state Construction Contractors Board. This notice can be in the form of a letter, but it must contain this information:

- The name and mailing address of the owner, or if the owner has a lawyer or other legal representative, the name and mailing address of that person
- A statement that the owner may bring a court action against the contractor (or compel arbitration if a written contract requires arbitration)
- The address of the home where the problem is
- A description of *each* defect, what the owner thinks must be done to fix it, any other damage caused by the work that can't be fixed, and
- Any report or other document that contains evidence of the defects and other damage. (Documents can include photographs, receipts for property showing the amount of damage done to possessions, reports about the defect created by official inspectors or other contractors, etc.)

In some situations, the contractor may have been at the mercy of a supplier who ran up the home owner's construction costs by not delivering needed materials timely or at all—or delivering defective or wrong materials. In such a case, the homeowner must send a "notice of defect" to the supplier at its

Oregon business address. If the supplier does not have an Oregon address, the notice must go to the supplier's registered agent (see Chapter 2 for more information.) The notice must contain all the points mentioned above for contractors. In some situations, the homeowner may have to send notices to both a contractor and a supplier.

The contractor or supplier has a right, but not a duty, to conduct a visual inspection of the home if he or she asks in writing to do so within 14 days after receiving the notice of defect. The response must estimate how much time the contractor will need to do the inspection. The contractor has a duty to forward the notice of defect to subcontractors and suppliers. Any of these workers has the right to inspect by asking the homeowner in writing within 14 days after the first contractor asked to inspect. These workers must specify whether they will do a visual inspection only, or an inspection that involves testing. The response must estimate how long the inspection and testing, if any, will take.

Whether or not the contractor or supplier decides to inspect, he or she must respond in writing to the owner's notice of defect within 90 days after receiving the notice. For *each* of the problems the owner outlined in the notice of defect and for any other problems the contractor or supplier noticed when inspecting, the response must include:

- Either a statement that the reported defect does not exist, or that the contractor or supplier agrees that the defect exists, along with the nature and extent of the defect
- A statement describing the existence of a defect related to or different from the reported defect, describing the nature or extent of the defect
- Copies of any reports made by an inspector in response to the homeowner's notice of defects

The contractor can offer to fix the problem or compensate the homeowner for the damage or defect. If the owner agrees that the proposed solution is acceptable, the owner must agree to it in writing within 30 days. If the proposal is not acceptable, the parties can continue to negotiate; the homeowner becomes eligible to take the contractor to small claims (or regular) court if

- The contractor or supplier does not respond to the notice of defect within the time allowed

- The response does not offer to repair the problem or compensate the homeowner
- The homeowner rejects an offer from the contractor or the supplier to repair the defect or compensate the homeowner for the damage
- The contractor or supplier doesn't follow through after the homeowner accepts an offer for repair or compensation

All of this correspondence can take time. How will it affect the time limit to sue? An owner who sends a notice of defects in the time allowed to start a court case has a longer time limit. It will be the latest date after

- 120 days after getting a written response from the contractor who doesn't offer to repair the problem or compensate the homeowner, or
- 120 days after the homeowner rejects an offer to repair or compensate, or
- 30 days after the date specified in an acceptance of a written offer to repair or compensate as the date by which the repair or compensation must be made.

A possible alternative to court is the complaint process available through the state's Construction Contractors Board. All contractors who register with the CCB must be bonded. In the event of a dispute about the quality or amount of work done by a registered contractor, a homeowner can ask the CCB for mediation. A homeowner who prevails in a CCB case can get compensation through the contractor's **bond**. For more information about the complaint process, see www.oregon.gov/CCB/complaints/Pages/how-file-a-complaint. aspx.

What a contractor can do

Most people—builders, landscapers, plumbers, electricians, etc.—who perform work on or around a person's home have the right to file a **construction lien** on real estate belonging to the homeowner. Once filed in the recorder's office in the county where the property is, the lien gives the contractor the right to be paid when the real estate is sold. Most homeowners don't want to have unnecessary liens on their land, so they are likely to pay to avoid one. If the lien is for more than $3,000, the contractor may be able to collect the debt by forcing the sale of the property. It's a step that the contractor can take only in circuit court, not in small claims court. It's not a sure way to get paid, either. If the real estate has other liens on it—for a mortgage, property taxes, other debts, etc.— those liens likely will have priority over the contractor's more recent lien. If the property is sold, those lien holders usually have the right to be paid off first. The last lienholder in line may find there is no money left from the proceeds of the sale after everyone else has gotten his or her share.

CONSUMER WARRANTIES

A merchant that sells, leases, or rents consumer products—things that people buy or lease for personal, family, or household use—has a legal duty to those who buy or lease the products. Every product comes with an "implied warranty" that the product is fit for normal uses. Some products come with written contracts that require the consumer to participate in mediation before or arbitration instead of going to court. Depending on the state law that applies to the contract, the consumer may not have to participate in arbitration (example: Oregon law does not prohibit arbitration in consumer cases; New Mexico law does). The contract itself normally will say which state's law will apply in the event of a dispute, and it doesn't have to be the law of the state where the consumer lives or even where the consumer signed the contract. An Oregon court will apply the law of whichever state the contract requires, unless the parties agree otherwise.

The problem: A consumer buys a product for household use that falls apart as the consumer is gently removing the product from its packaging, or as the consumer is using the product in a normal or reasonably foreseeable manner during the warranty period.

The consumer plaintiff must establish:

- Plaintiff purchased or rented product that did not work properly within the warranty period
- Plaintiff was using the product in a normal or reasonably foreseeable manner
- Product was defective

Plaintiff's proof: testimony about price, type of product, time of purchase, use of product at time defect occurred or appeared; expert testimony if needed, about construction defects, foreseeable uses of product; written contract, if any; product itself if product can be brought into courtroom or, if not, photos of product

Defendant's possible defenses:

- Plaintiff had duty to arbitrate or mediate and did not do it
- Plaintiff gave no notice of breach of warranty
- Warranty period over at time problem arose
- Plaintiff misused product
- Defendant not a merchant as defined by law
- Too late to file case against defendant

Defendant's proof: testimony about whether defendant is merchant, contacts with plaintiff about product defect, plaintiff misuse of product; written contract, language relating to arbitration or mediation requirements.

Some products come with an additional warranty, called a warranty of fitness for a particular purpose. Sometimes this warranty is in writing: for example, "This jack is made to jack up vehicles of up to 12,000 lbs." Or, "These snow tires will not skid even on windy mountain roads covered with black ice." But sometimes this kind of warranty is oral only. If you're nervously examining a mini-van at a used car lot, and you ask the salesperson, "Is this car good?" and the salesperson says, "It's a great little van," you probably haven't gotten the salesperson to make a warranty of fitness for a particular purpose. But if you ask him or her, "Can I count on this van to get me from Grants Pass to Cave Junction every day for my job?," you've asked a specific question about what the car can be relied on to do. If the salesperson replies, "Absolutely! You should have no trouble with this car's getting you to work," the salesperson has just warranted that the car is fit for the particular purpose of getting you reliably to your job 30 miles away. You buy the van based on what the salesperson has told you. If you see black smoke belching from the tailpipe two weeks after you buy this car, you likely have a claim against the seller under the "particular purpose" warranty—assuming you can prove in court that the salesperson said what you claim. (Hint: Never go to a used-car dealership without an attentive witness at your side!)

Problem: Plaintiff bought car from Fiendish Motors after being assured the car would get her reliably to her job 40 miles away.

Plaintiff must establish:

- Plaintiff bought car for specific purpose
- Seller knew what the specific purpose was
- Seller made assurances about suitability of car for that purpose
- Plaintiff relied on seller's assurances
- Car was in fact not suitable for the intended purpose

Plaintiff's proof: testimony about transaction and reliance on assurances as basis for making purchase; possible testimony of expert witness about ease of discovering defect, nature of defect; maintenance records, any language in contract or other document showing assurances about suitability for purpose

Defendant's possible defenses:

- Defendant did not know or have any reason to know specific purpose for purchase
- Buyer did not rely on seller's statements as basis for purchase
- Plaintiff misused product, causing product defect or failure (for example, seller told buyer that car had slight oil leak; buyer did not check oil for two months, and all oil drained out of engine)
- Too late for plaintiff to sue

Defendant's proof: testimony of salesperson about transaction; written contract showing no assurances, date of transaction

Defective products—strict liability

The problem: Consumer bought a new product for normal household or family use. During normal use, the product shatters/explodes/catches fire/ strangles a small child/poisons a user/causes some other kind of harm

Plaintiff must establish:

- Plaintiff purchased or leased product from merchant.
- Product was unreasonably dangerous at the time of purchase or lease
- Manufacturer and/or merchant had duty to warn about unreasonable

risk, or to manufacture product using a safer design or components

- Plaintiff or family or household member was injured by the product
- Amount of damages (medical, rehabilitation, loss of income, etc.)

Plaintiff's proof: plaintiff's testimony about problem, age of product, use of product, harm caused, amount of damages; expert witness testimony about risks and dangers in product, comparison with similar products, normal and foreseeable uses of product

Defendant's possible defenses:

- Defendant did not manufacture or sell product in question
- Defendant not merchant or manufacturer (example: plaintiff bought product used, at a garage sale held by defendant)
- Plaintiff's use of product is completely outside of scope of reasonably foreseeable or normal uses
- Plaintiff did not properly maintain product
- Defendant placed appropriate warnings on product
- Manufacturer defense: product reached consumer only after someone made significant changes in the product
- Plaintiff waited too long to sue

Defendant's proof: testimony of manufacturer, designer, distributor, expert witness about product design and testing, visible warnings on product, foreseeable uses, product not made or distributed by defendant; contracts, warranties, other documents

CHILDREN'S MEDICAL EXPENSES

When parents divorce, get a legal separation, or a judgment of custody for children, the circuit court judgment in their case will normally say who will be responsible for child support and how the parents will allocate the costs of medical care for the children. At the time of the judgment, no one knows how much those costs will be, so the court leaves it up to the parents to follow the court order in the future. After the judgment is entered, however, one parent may find that he or she is the only one paying for the children's medical treatment even though the judgment says the other parent must pay all or a portion of those costs. The parent who is paying has the right under the judgment to go to small claims (or circuit) court to get a judgment against the parent who is supposed to be paying. The plaintiff must show the amount of medical care he or she paid for, along with the language in the court judgment showing how much the other parent is liable for. A parent can go to court each time the obligated parent fails to pay, or periodically go to court for a judgment against the other parent as the bills add up over time. As in every other kind of small claim case, the plaintiff must make a pre-filing attempt to get the other parent to pay, by showing the obligated parent copies of the bills the plaintiff paid and asking for reimbursement.

DEBTS FROM A MARRIAGE OR DOMESTIC PARTNERSHIP

When spouses or partners stop living together as a household and start taking responsibility for only their own expenses, they don't have any liability for the new expenses of the other spouse or partner. In most cases, however, they remain responsible for each other's debts incurred during their marriage or civil union from before they started living apart. (There are some exceptions to this rule; talk to a family law attorney for specific advice about your situation.) When they get a court judgment that makes them officially single, that judgment will usually say who will be responsible for which debts they incurred while together.

Unfortunately, the court judgment doesn't have any effect on the rights of creditors unless the creditors expressly agree they will pursue only one of the parties. (Such agreements rarely happen; if you are lucky enough to get a creditor to agree in your situation, get the agreement in writing!) If one ex-spouse or ex-partner doesn't pay those creditors, they can come after the other "ex." If you are the person who isn't obligated to pay a certain debt according to the divorce judgment, you can give the creditors that information—but they will be more interested in finding out how they can get payment. You can offer to help by letting them know where your "ex" works or has bank accounts or other assets, but you may not be able to persuade them not to sue you instead of or in addition to that person. If the creditor is a professional debt collector and the debt is a consumer debt, you may have one or more defenses based on unlawful methods of collection (see ORS 646.639 for a list of unlawful practices). You also have a defense against paying if your "ex" incurred the debt after you were physically separated. (If you separated more than once, only the final one counts as protection from the other person's individual debts.) For that reason, it can be important to document when you started living apart, as you will need to provide evidence of your separation.

If you are the person who hasn't been paying and your "ex" is hounding you for the money, you may think that his or her debt collection efforts are unlawful. The protections of the consumer debt collection laws do not apply to people who aren't engaged in the *business* of collecting debts, however.

DEBTS OF PEOPLE WHO LIVE TOGETHER INFORMALLY

As a general rule, people who live together but are not married or in a civil union are not responsible for debts incurred at any time by their partners. The main exception is if both people signed a contract (for a loan, a joint credit card, purchases of consumer goods, etc.) with the creditor. Anyone who signs a contract is liable for a valid debt, regardless of his or her marital status.

CO-SIGNERS AND CONTRACTS

Anyone who signs a contract as a co-signer is just as liable for the debt as the primary signer is. The co-signer who is taken to court by a creditor has all of the defenses the primary signer has. If the debt is a consumer debt and the collector has engaged in any unlawful collection practices against the co-signer, he or she can raise that conduct as a defense and as a counterclaim.

SHODDY SERVICES—contract and tort

Most people have had at least one bad experience with someone—private or professional—who provides services:

- Plaintiff goes to a hair salon for a permanent, leaves with burned/straight/green/no hair.
- Plaintiff leaves item at pawn shop, and, returning to get it back, learns that pawnbroker mistakenly gave the item to another customer.

- Plaintiff takes green silk dress to drycleaner, and gets back a green-and-white splattered silk dress.
- Plaintiff takes car to dealer for oil change—and discovers too late that dealer forgot to replace oil.
- Plaintiff hires a seamstress to make a wedding dress—that doesn't fit.

These examples all involve breaches of contracts: a customer hires someone to perform a service in a professional manner, and the person hired for the job gets it wrong. They may also involve negligence on the part of the person who got it wrong. Chapter 9 will look at these examples of contract-based problems that involve negligence, along with cases that have nothing to do with contracts, such as traffic accidents, drug-dealing neighbors, and vandalism.

CHAPTER 9

Making your case, part 3: Tort cases

Chapter 8 looked at some typical breach-of-contract claims. This chapter looks at tort claims. Sometimes a single case can have a claim for breach of contract *and* a claim under tort law. Does that matter? Sometimes.

It doesn't matter at the time you are filing your case: your claim form simply needs to tell the court and the defendant that you expect the defendant to pay you damages, reimburse you, or return something that belongs to you. (See sample claim forms at the end of Chapter 3.) When you are preparing for court, though, you may find it helpful to have more than one way to present your side of the case.

General elements of negligence claims

Think about the three examples at the end of Chapter 8—the hairdresser who fries your hair, the drycleaner who somehow bleaches color out of your silk dress, the auto mechanic who forgets to replace the oil in your car. You entered into a contract with them to do something for you in exchange for payment. If they didn't do the work, they breached the contract. In addition, in all of these business-and-consumer relationships, they had a duty to care for your hair, your car, your dress properly. In each of these examples, they've done it wrong— probably because they weren't careful. They were negligent. Negligence of this kind is a tort. Like a breach of contract, negligence has certain elements that you should be prepared to prove in court.

113

The elements of negligence are fairly straightforward:

- Someone owes you a duty to be reasonably careful in a particular situation
- The person isn't careful enough
- Not being careful creates a foreseeable risk of harm
- The carelessness actually causes you that kind of harm

You can see that these elements apply to bad-hair experiences, improper auto repair, bad dry cleaning, and medical and other professional malpractice—all situations that came out of contracts you entered into with the defendants.

The problem: Licensed hairdresser gives customer a permanent, using her usual product, "Goldie's Never-Fail" permanent wave solution. When hairdresser washes out that new permanent wave, the customer sees that her hair is fried to a crisp. She paid $90 for the treatment. She then goes to another hairdresser, who cuts and treats her hair to try to save it, paying another $110. Despite the best possible "repair," the hair is fuzzy, thinner, and discolored.

Plaintiff customer must establish:

- Plaintiff had hair that seemed normal before seeing defendant, a licensed hair professional, for a permanent
- Plaintiff's hair was damaged by the treatment
- Plaintiff paid $90 for the treatment, then $110 to another hairdresser to repair the damage

Plaintiff's proof: testimony and testimony of second hairdresser; usage information and instructions for product; photos of hair before permanent, after permanent, and after repairs by second hairdresser; proof of payment or estimate of cost to repair damage

Defendant hairdresser's possible defenses:

- Plaintiff had previously treated hair and did not tell hairdresser about chemicals already present in hair that hairdresser would not otherwise know about
- Plaintiff ordered hairdresser to perform treatment differently from the normal approved method

Defendant's proof: testimony about experience with customer, product used, and possible expert testimony from other hairdresser familiar with product; written instructions for use accompanying product; list of ingredients in product; cost to hairdresser of product; hairdresser's offer to repair damage to hair at no additional charge (thus saving plaintiff $110)

In a case like this one, you can see the possibility of other kinds of damages, too. If the plaintiff is a professional who is a newscaster on television or who makes presentations to industry groups, for example, the plaintiff may decide that the only way she can look professional is by wearing a wig for these events until her hair grows back. In an extreme case, the cost of a wig would be appropriate. If the plaintiff is a photographer's model, she may lose modeling jobs while her hair grows back. Those lost jobs can also be considered damages.

Negligence can be the basis for a claim in cases that don't involve contracts, too, such as traffic accidents. Traffic accidents are another common type of case that ends up in small claims court.

TRAFFIC ACCIDENTS

In a typical traffic accident involving two vehicles, one driver is likely to be at fault. If the police respond, they may issue a citation to that driver. There may be damage to one or both cars, and possibly damage to property (stop signs, light poles, fences, etc.). A driver or passenger may have been injured, incurring ambulance, hospital, and medical expenses.

Oregon law requires all parties to an accident to notify their insurance companies whenever they are involved in an accident. Generally, the insurance companies will try to negotiate a settlement of the case. Don't file a small claims case about the accident while they are still negotiating! There is no purpose in going to court if your claim will be dealt with by insurers. If you lose the court case, the insurance company that might have paid you for your loss won't do so now.

Note: You can decide whether to accept it or reject any offer an insurance company makes to you. Get some legal advice when you are deciding what to do, as a personal injury or other tort lawyer will usually have a pretty good idea

115

of what your case is worth. If your expectations are unrealistic, you want to find that out before you reject a reasonable offer and file a court case.

The problem: A driver runs a stop sign at an intersection, ramming the side of the plaintiff's car. Police cite the driver. Plaintiff has temporary neck pain caused by the accident. She spends $900 on chiropractic care. She misses three days of work as a result of the accident, losing $500 in wages. She gets three estimates on the cost of repairing and repainting her passenger car door. The estimates range from $1300 to $1700. She rejects an offer from the driver's insurance company for $2200.

Plaintiff must establish:

- Defendant driver had duty to drive safely
- Defendant violated that duty, and state law, by failing to stop at a stop sign
- As a result of failing to stop lawfully, defendant drove into the side of plaintiff's car
- Plaintiff was injured, she lost wages while getting treated for her injuries, and her car was damaged, and the amounts she claims for each cost

Plaintiff's proof: testimony and testimony of witnesses to accident and police; photos of scene, diagrams, police report

Defendant's possible defenses:

- Plaintiff also was negligent (driving too fast)
- Defendant stopped at stop sign
- Defendant attempted to stop, but brakes unexpectedly gave out, or gravel on road caused car to slide, or oil or grease had been spilled on road, etc., making it impossible to stop even after proper braking
- Plaintiff was in better position to prevent accident
- Emergency
- Plaintiff's damage claim is excessive
- Plaintiff waited too long to file her case

Defendant's proof: testimony about plaintiff's fault, testimony of police; testimony of mechanic, other witnesses at scene about brakes, road condition; estimates for repairs

Can the defendant win the case by claiming the plaintiff was also at fault in the collision? In some cases, yes (although probably not this one). Imagine that the defendant didn't stop at the stop sign because he saw the plaintiff driving fast toward his car, and he reasonably believed that he and others would be safer if he tried to move past the plaintiff's fast-approaching car to avert a collision. Those facts would suggest that plaintiff is at least as responsible for the collision as defendant is.

CONTRIBUTORY AND COMPARATIVE NEGLIGENCE

What would happen in the case of an accident where both drivers are at fault? The court must decide who was more at fault. If the plaintiff seemed more at fault than the defendant, the plaintiff should lose the case. If the plaintiff seemed not at all at fault, the plaintiff should win the case. If the plaintiff is partly at fault, and the defendant is more at fault, the court should reduce what the plaintiff wins by the plaintiff's proportion of the fault. In a case in which the plaintiff claims and documents $2000 in damages in a negligence case, a judge might find that the defendant was 70 per cent at fault and the plaintiff 30 per cent at fault. So the judge would reduce the plaintiff's win by 30 per cent; she could get a judgment of up to $1400 (70 per cent of what she was claiming).

In some cases, a traffic accident may involve several vehicles and drivers. If you are a potential plaintiff, think carefully before your file your case about how much of the fault for the accident might have been yours. If you believe that the other drivers were more at fault, make sure to name them all as defendants.

Important: If you can't give personal service of your claim to a defendant who is registered as a driver with the Oregon DMV in this kind of case, you must mail a copy to any address the defendant gave you at the scene of the accident; any address you are aware of that has a reasonable chance of reaching the defendant; and the last known address of the defendant shown in the driving records of the Oregon Department of Transportation.

MEDICAL/DENTAL/LEGAL/PROFESSIONAL MALPRACTICE

The problem: Plaintiff paid his CPA $900 to research a tax issue for him. The CPA made an educated guess about what the answer to the tax question was, without actually looking up the relevant rules. The CPA could have and should have learned that the rules had changed nine months earlier. The advice the CPA gave cost the plaintiff $7,950 in tax penalties and fees.

Plaintiff must establish:

- Plaintiff was a client of the CPA
- The CPA didn't apply the level of professional skill the client had the right to expect, because the CPA didn't perform the basic research needed to determine what the applicable tax rule was
- The CPA's carelessness was the direct cause of plaintiff's loss of $7,950

Plaintiff's proof: plaintiff's testimony, testimony of a different CPA about the care a non-negligent CPA would use (unless the error is really blatant); documents from IRS, state taxation and revenue department, bill and relevant correspondence from CPA defendant

Defendant's possible defenses:

- Plaintiff was not a client but merely an acquaintance who asked for offhand information
- The CPA used the level of skill the plaintiff had the right to expect
- All clients are responsible themselves for decisions they make about their tax liability
- Plaintiff waited too long to file case

Defendant's proof: CPA's testimony and testimony of other CPA; disclaimer of liability on report to client (Note to plaintiff: Just because a defendant says he's not liable doesn't make it so.)

Use this same general approach with a medical malpractice claim. Be aware that the standard of care for doctors and other medical professionals can vary from one location to another. For example, in the Portland metro area, radiologists believe it is very important to compare past mammograms with new ones, as changes in the picture can signal a problem. In at least one rural Oregon community, radiologists generally don't bother to make the comparison. In short: potential plaintiffs who question the quality of medical care they received in another part of the state need to consider that what a specialist in Portland tells them is malpractice may not be malpractice by the standards that apply in Wagon Tire or Shady Cove or Lakeview or Cave Junction.

What about legal malpractice? The general approach is the same, but there is one large obstacle to overcome. Not only do you have to show that the lawyer did something wrong (conducting no or inadequate research, missing deadlines, waiting too long to file the case, etc.), you have to persuade the court that the case the lawyer accepted from you was so good you would have won it but for the lawyer's malpractice.

A legal malpractice problem sometimes involves a lawyer's violation of the Oregon State Bar rules of ethics. Be sure to contact the Oregon State Bar Association to find out how to file a complaint, and also how to reach the bar's malpractice insurance provider, the Professional Liability Fund. The bar investigates each complaint thoroughly. In a few cases where malpractice is obvious, it is able to reimburse or partially reimburse clients for losses they suffered at the hands of incompetent or unethical attorneys.

Intentional Torts

Assault, battery, stalking, libel, slander, conversion, and vandalism are all examples of intentional torts. They are not "accidents." The elements of libel and slander are listed in Chapter 7.

__ASSAULT, BATTERY__

Oregon law doesn't always make a clear distinction between an assault--an unsuccessful attempt to push, hurt, shove, shoot, stab, burn, or otherwise harm someone—and a battery, the harm itself. Therefore, plaintiffs must describe very clearly what the defendant did. As described here, assault and battery can mean physical contact between the assailant and the victim. It can also mean an attack by the use of objects such as guns, thrown cell phones, and shopping carts or other objects used as battering rams. Below is an example of an indirect battery like these.

The problem: After boss fired employee for frequent absences, ex- employee waited outside for boss to get into her car, then rammed it with his own car.

Plaintiff must establish:

- Defendant knew she was in her car
- Defendant intentionally drove his car into hers
- She was frightened, injured, etc., by the conduct
- She incurred bills for treatment and car repairs, for which defendant should pay

Plaintiff's proof: plaintiff's testimony, testimony of witnesses; bills for treatment and repairs, photos of damage, police reports

Defendant's possible defenses:

- Car went out of control
- Defendant did not know plaintiff was in car, so not responsible for medical bills or emotional distress damages
- Plaintiff misidentified him as the culprit
- Plaintiff drove at his car and he acted in self-defense

Defendant's proof: testimony, testimony of expert about car malfunction, testimony of witnesses as to his whereabouts; police reports

CONVERSION (theft)

Conversion resembles the general crime of theft. It includes not just taking something without the owner's consent but also borrowing something and then refusing to give it back.

The problem: Plaintiff's neighbor likes plaintiff's riding lawn mower. The mower disappears in the fall. In the spring, plaintiff sees neighbor using the mower on his own lawn, and demands it back. Neighbor refuses to return the machine.

Plaintiff must establish:

- Property belongs to plaintiff

- Defendant has property and refuses to return it
- Value of property

Plaintiff's proof: testimony; proof of purchase or other proof of ownership, value of property

Defendant's possible defenses

- Property did not belong to plaintiff
- Plaintiff gave defendant property as gift
- Property had no monetary value

VANDALISM—DAMAGE TO PROPERTY

Vandalism is intentional damage to property. (It's different from the damage associated with a traffic accident, where someone has *carelessly* hit a pole, a post, a fence, or a structure.) It includes destruction and graffiti "tagging". In criminal court, this conduct is known as "criminal mischief."

The problem: Pastor orders three teenaged boys out of the church parking lot where they have been practicing fast starts with their junker car. That night, a neighbor sees three youths defacing the sign on the church lawn, and the next day a church member tells the pastor that the boys were bragging at school about the vandalism. The church member tells the pastor who the culprits are.

Plaintiff must establish:

- Damage to private property
- Damage was not accidental
- Defendants are responsible for damage
- Amount of damages to reimburse for repairs

Plaintiff's proof: testimony of witnesses, plaintiff himself or herself; photos; bill for repairs.

In the above example, the defendants are minors. For that reason, the plaintiff must name not only the juveniles as defendants but also their custodial parents, who are responsible for up to $7,500 in damages.

Defendants' possible defenses:

- Defendants not responsible for damage
- Damage accidental, not intentional
- Amount of damages claimed excessive

Defendant's proof: testimony of defendant and witnesses; evidence of reasonable cost of repairs

NUISANCE

Anything that occurs on someone else's property but that significantly interferes with your ability to use and enjoy your property can be a **nuisance**. A nuisance can be a **public nuisance**, one that affects everyone around it in the same general way. An example of this kind of nuisance would be the opening of a stock car race track in a residential neighborhood. Suddenly everyone who lives there is bombarded with the smell of burning rubber and the screech of brakes for hours at a time, the roar of crowds, and an enormous increase in the amount of traffic in the neighborhood. The resale value of homes in this neighborhood suffers. While it's possible for an individual to sue in a public nuisance case, it makes more sense for the affected neighbors to take their complaints to local officials, who can then negotiate with the offender to address the complaints.

There's also **private nuisance**. This type of nuisance has a particular impact on only one or a few people. Using the race track example above, the family who lives right next door to the entrance experiences all the annoyance that the neighbors do. In addition, though, this family finds beer cans, potato chip and gum wrappers, cigarette butts and empty cigarette packs, race sheets, and other debris all over its front yard, because patrons of the race track leave a trail of garbage behind them when they enter and leave the track area.

Some other examples of private nuisance:

- Your neighbor decides to become a dog breeder. Soon you are serenaded by seven barking dogs all day long. The dog feces bring swarms of flies and wasps into the area, along with a nasty stench. You can't go outside without holding your breath. At night, any noise in the neighborhood brings about a 20-minute baying frenzy. You can't get a decent night's sleep.

- A heavy metal band sets up its rehearsal studio across the street. The band practices from 10 p.m. to 5 a.m. daily. You really, really can't get a decent night's sleep.
- Your next-door neighbor has vowed to use only natural products to fertilize her garden this year. You are unhappy to see, and smell, a huge pile of fresh manure in her back yard. When she applies stinky fish emulsion to her happy plants, you are even more dismayed. You can no longer sit on your patio or barbecue in your back yard. You must keep your doors and windows closed to escape the smell all spring and summer.

Getting into a dispute with neighbors is not something anyone wants to do. In some cases, the neighbor may not realize that the noisy dogs and the stinky garden are a problem for others, and the person will take steps to stop the annoyance. In other cases, the problem neighbor may not care how others are affected. If it's a tenant who is creating the nuisance, annoyed neighbors will have to sue the owner of the property if the renter won't address the problem. In some cases, the conduct may even be illegal. If court becomes necessary,

Plaintiff must establish:

- Nearby property is the source of a nuisance
- Defendant is owner (or part owner) of property that is the source of the nuisance
- Nuisance has interfered with plaintiff's ability to make normal use of his or her own property, causing inconvenience, distress, danger, lack of sleep, accumulation of garbage, excessive noise, etc.
- Amount of damages as result of interference and/or
- Court should force defendant to stop nuisance behavior—*nuisance cases are the only ones in which small claims court has the authority to enjoin bad behavior. Some judges may not know this.*

Plaintiff's proof: testimony of plaintiff, other nearby neighbors or visitors; records of police involvement, if any; photographs of trash or dangerous objects; recordings of excessive noise, etc.

Defendant's possible defenses:

- Defendant promptly addressed plaintiff's complaints, so plaintiff has no damages
- Plaintiff has not experienced interference with normal enjoyment of property
- It is not possible to operate defendant's lawful business without the disturbance plaintiff complained about (Neighborhood taverns are immune from this kind of claim!)
- Plaintiff has waited too long to file claim

Defendant's proof: testimony of defendant, other neighbors; records of complaints, police involvement

THE DANGEROUS NUISANCE—drug houses

What can be done about the new neighbor who is a drug dealer? You and others on your street watch in horror as he welcomes customers, lots of them, well into the night. Sometimes there are shouts and threats, and you soon see used syringes and other drug paraphernalia on the ground. You know this trash can be dangerous, especially for children and pets. If the dealer is a renter, you first complain to the owner, who says he doesn't care.

Now what? In the case of the drug dealer next door, it can be difficult for one plaintiff to have an impact—or avoid an ugly aftermath—with a small claims case. It's important to have all the other neighbors on board, first by forming an active Neighborhood Watch that alerts police to activities at the property, and second, if necessary, by filing separate nuisance claims against the owner of the property all at one time. If the dealer is a renter, the owner should finally figure out that he needs to care about the neighbors and evict the problem tenant. If the owner still doesn't act, or if the dealer is the owner, plaintiffs who prove damage claims can place liens on the property. See Chapter 11 for more information on liens. If the court grants an injunction against the nuisance, the neighbors will have to go to circuit court if the defendant violates the injunction—but they can pool their funds to hire one lawyer.

TRESPASS

When someone or something comes onto your property without your consent, that action is known as trespass. A hunter may climb over the fence onto your land; a neighbor's horses may break down their own fence and come to your house to sample your prize roses. Someone who lives up the hill may divert a creek, with the result that rain forms a new waterway that later floods your back yard. Trespass even includes a neighbor's use of sprayed pesticides that find their way into your yard. For all of these situations,

Plaintiff must establish:

- Plaintiff gave notice forbidding entry onto the land (by posting the land, by installing and maintaining fences, notifying defendant personally, etc.)
- Defendant or something belonging to defendant came onto plaintiff's land
- Plaintiff was harmed as a result of invasion—loss of privacy, actual damages in the form of harm, if any, to the land itself
- Amount of damages

Plaintiff's proof: testimony about notice and invasion; testimony of expert (about changes in water courses, etc); photos of trespass; bills, other costs

Defendant's possible defenses:

- No notice that entry is forbidden
- Emergency
- Adverse possession (the defendant claims the land as his own after many years of use, in limited situations)
- Trespassing animals not owned by defendant
- Changes in water courses, etc., not created by defendant

Defendant's proof: testimony about lack of signs, fences, other notice from plaintiff, ownership of animals; photos, other documentation

TORT CLAIMS AGAINST THE GOVERNMENT

Government agencies have limited liability for some kinds of torts. The "agency" can be a state government, a state board or commission, local government, irrigation and school districts, housing authorities, and some non-profits that get more than half of their funding from the state, such as some public transportation services, residential training facilities, and child care agencies. (There is also a federal tort claims act, which has very different rules; it is much more difficult to win a federal tort claim case. Those cases are not discussed here; talk to an attorney if you want more information about the federal law.)

An agency can commit a tort by failing to perform legally required services or failing to take steps to protect the public. **Some examples:**

- A community-operated water department has a duty to ensure that water is fit for normal uses.
- Transit authorities have a duty to hire safe drivers and to maintain equipment so it is safe for transport.
- Jails have a duty to keep inmates' belongings safe until the inmate leaves the jail. They also have a duty to keep inmates safe.
- Support enforcement agencies have a duty to collect an appropriate amount of child support from absent parents.
- Child protection services have a duty to investigate and monitor potentially dangerous living situations for children.
- If a hearing officer or judge orders an agency to do something, the agency has a duty to follow the order given.
- Street and highway departments must place and maintain roads and bridges and post warnings at dangerous intersections.

Agencies have insurance coverage in the event that the agencies commit a tort or their employees commit a tort while performing their prescribed duties. An employee who causes harm while acting outside the scope of the work he or she is supposed to be doing for the agency will not have the protection of this insurance. In a case in which an employee is clearly acting outside the scope of duty, it is appropriate to file against the employee, but not the agency. It can sometimes be difficult to tell whether an employee is acting within the scope of assigned duties. For example, police officers have the right to use force in carrying out their duties. They cannot use force that is excessive under the circumstances, however.

Before taking a state or local agency to small claims court with a tort claim, the plaintiff must give formal written notice to the agency. The notice must be received by the proper office within 180 days of the tort. There's a 90-day extension for someone who is too severely injured to give notice, or who is a minor or who lacks capacity in some other way. In a few cases, the plaintiff may need to give notice to other offices or agencies, too; this section does not address those additional requirements.

If the claim is against the state or an officer or employee of the state, the notice must go to the Oregon Department of Administrative Services. If the claim is against a local public body or one of its officers or employees, the claim must go to the public body at its main administrative office, or to an attorney who serves as general counsel to the public body. It is possible for an agency to get **actual notice** of a claim, too, which happens when informal communication with the agency should make the agency realize that someone intends to assert a claim. Unfortunately, the plaintiff must establish as part of the claim that he or she either gave notice within the time limit or that the agency had actual notice during the time limit. It can be difficult to prove that the agency received actual notice, however; relying on a formal writing is a much better approach. The plaintiff must keep a copy of the notice, along with proof of when it was delivered or sent.

The notice must contain very specific information:

- That plaintiff is asserting a claim for damages against the agency, or an officer, employee, or agent of the agency
- A description of the time, place, and circumstances that gave rise to the claim, to the best of the plaintiff's knowledge
- The name of the plaintiff and plaintiff's mailing address

The agency or its insurer may or may not respond. Keep any response you get as further proof that the agency received the notice. Sometimes the agency will agree that it did the wrong thing and will work with you to solve the problem informally, so that you will not have to go to court after all.

If you do wind up in court, the way to establish your case is to show that the agency had a duty to do something and didn't do it, or that it did something it didn't have the legal authority to do. Look at the sections above on negligence and traffic accidents for guidance. Remember that you also have to say that you gave the proper notice within the time limit.

TORT CLAIMS AND PRISONERS

There are special notice requirements that a prisoner in an Oregon jail or prison must follow when filing a tort claim against an agency in small claims court. Not only must the prisoner give the pre-filing tort claim notice, he or she must also give the agency extra time to respond to a filed claim and to the plaintiff's request for a default judgment in the case if the agency doesn't file an answer by the original deadline. The requirements apply whether the prisoner is in custody following a conviction or simply awaiting trial. First, the prisoner must change the claim form to allow 30 days, not just 15 days, for the agency to respond. After starting the case, the prisoner must send copies of *all* documents he or she files with the court to the agency, too. If the defendant is a state agency, or if the defendant is the Oregon Department of Corrections, the inmate must also serve copies of all court filings on the Oregon Attorney General. If the agency does not respond to the filing of the lawsuit within 30 days, the plaintiff must allow 10 days after seeking a default judgment for the agency to respond. The plaintiff must give the state notice that he or she is seeking the order of default, too. Only if the agency does not respond at this point can the court sign an order of default and a judgment against the agency.

Either the agency or the Attorney General can have the case transferred to a circuit court. The plaintiff then has 20 days in which to re-file in circuit court, as described in Chapter 3. Whether or not the case gets transferred, the agency has the right to send an attorney or paralegal from the state Department of Justice to represent the agency at trial.

128

CHAPTER 10

Your day in court

Your research, your investigation, and your efforts to settle your dispute all have prepared you to present your case in small claims court. Today is the day: *now* what do you do?

You know it is important to look respectful and "respectable". You know it is important to appear reasonable. It's also very important to be in the courtroom on time. If you arrive late, you may be *too* late; the judge will already have ruled for the other side in your absence. That advice may seem obvious, but people unfamiliar with the courthouse underestimate how much time it takes to get where they need to be:

- First, if you're driving to court and your car has been known to die in the middle of the street, you may want to use someone else's car—but only if it's more reliable! Either leave for court really early or make sure to have backup transportation.
- Second, finding parking near the courthouse can be tough. Allow for time to walk several blocks to the courthouse. And don't gamble on a short-term parking meter. Although your trial notice might say your case starts at 1:30 p.m., all of the day's small claims trials are set for the same time, and the cases are heard one after another. You don't want to worry about getting a ticket or having your car towed while you are waiting for your hearing.
- Third, once you get to the courthouse, you will need to pass through a security screening. This process takes time. You may be asked to take off jewelry, belts, and shoes. Some courthouses do not permit cell

129

phones or recording or transmitting devices. None permit weapons (including things like mace or pepper spray) of any kind; some will keep such things permanently. Leave at home anything that might keep you from getting into the building. Note: You might have physical exhibits for your case that the screeners will not allow you to take past security. If that happens, ask them to hold the items for your court hearing; then, when you get into the courtroom, tell the courtroom clerk that the security screeners have your evidence. The clerk will arrange for the items to be brought to the courtroom.

- Finally, once you are inside the building, you may have to find your courtroom if it's not listed on your trial notice and if you can't get the information by phone from the small claims clerk's office ahead of time. Some courthouses have video displays of the names of people with cases that day, showing the room number. Some have paper lists of case names tacked to a bulletin board. In some courthouses, you will have to ask a security guard, an information desk attendant, or someone in the civil case clerk's office where you are supposed to go. Expect to spend time waiting in line. If you plan to use witnesses in your case, be sure they know about the need to arrive early, too, and how to find the right courtroom.

- Lawyers often arrange to meet with their clients and all witnesses at the courthouse well before trial starts, to make sure everyone shows up (and to find and remind those who haven't shown up) and go over everyone's testimony one last time. You may want to do the same thing.

In the courtroom

When you enter the courtroom, you likely will see a dozen or more people—parties in other cases, witnesses, and observers. An assistant to the judge may ask you who you are and whether you have any witnesses who will testify, or may simply call out the names of the cases to be heard. If the assistant does not call out your name with the other case names, alert him or her immediately so the judge will know your case is set for hearing. Have your case number ready to make it easier to find your file.

Everyone must stand when the judge enters the courtroom and remain standing until the judge says people can sit down. The judge then will announce the name of the first case to be heard. When it's your turn, everyone in your case that you named as a plaintiff should approach the front of the room and stand behind the lawyers' table to their right. Everyone who is named as a defendant should stand behind the other table. (If the other side goes to "your" table, just take the other one. Also, some judges may direct you to a particular table.) Do not sit down until the judge gives permission to do so, usually right after the judge or the assistant swears in all the parties. When you start to talk, the clerk or the judge will ask you to state your name and to spell your last name for the official record. Every other witness must do the same thing when starting to testify. One of the plaintiffs should introduce the other plaintiffs—by full name, not "This is my husband." When it is time for the defendants to talk, one of them should introduce the others.

All parties and witnesses must agree to be sworn in or affirm that they will tell "the truth, the whole truth, and nothing but the truth." Sometimes everyone involved in all the cases for the day will be sworn in at one time before the hearings even start.

Unless they are named as one of the parties, witnesses should not sit at the table with you. In fact, either side can ask the judge to keep all witnesses completely outside the courtroom ("exclude witnesses") until it is time for them to testify. The purpose is to help witnesses testify based solely on their own knowledge and not merely repeat what the party or another witness has said. Although you don't have to ask for witnesses to be excluded until it's their turn to testify, some people find it's a good idea. The judge will always grant this request. Some judges require witnesses to wait outside even if the parties don't ask.

The hearing process

In each case, the judge will expect the plaintiff to talk first, explaining the reason for the lawsuit and presenting evidence that supports his or her position. While a formal court proceeding usually involves opening statements and closing arguments when attorneys are involved, there is no need for these formalities in small claims court; many judges don't even allow them.

The parties are allowed to talk only to the judge during the hearing, without any side conversation with the opposing party. Neither side is allowed to interrupt the other side's presentation. The judge, however, is free to ask questions of you as you present your case.

After the defendant has spoken, the judge *may* ask the plaintiff to respond. Plaintiffs shouldn't count on getting this opportunity, however. In fact, both sides should always tell the whole story when it's their turn to talk; they may not get an opportunity to add important information later. If, after the other side's presentation, you have important information to add, ask the judge if you can speak again if the judge does not invite you to speak.

As a defendant, your job is to show the court why the plaintiff isn't entitled to what he or she is asking for in the claim. The judge will tell you when it is time to start your side of the case. If you have filed a counterclaim, the judge may want you to discuss it at the same time you talk about your defenses to the lawsuit. If not, don't forget to talk about the counterclaim later! (Remember you have to bring up all the elements of your claim; although it will seem odd, repeating some of the facts of the plaintiff's claim against you may be necessary to cover those elements.)

Basic courtroom manners

This book has already mentioned that it's a bad idea to go into court appearing hostile or angry. Remember that what you are doing is a form of salesmanship— you want the judge to "buy" your side of the story. Judges expect people not to wear hats or chew gum or tobacco in the courtroom. Violate these rules and you will get the kind of attention you don't want when you are trying to make a good impression.

Even if you say "Yeah" and "Hunh?" to everyone you know, it's much better form in court to say "Yes, judge" or "Yes, your honor" and "Pardon?" And acting out is bound to hurt your chances: glaring, eye rolling, interrupting, slamming down documents, sarcasm, and dramatic sighs are all extremely inappropriate. You may have been screened for weapons at the courthouse entrance—but you can still shoot yourself in the foot with this kind of behavior.

Presenting your evidence

A basic rule of the courtroom is that the judge cannot consider any information that is not admitted into evidence. Testimony is one kind of evidence. In some small claims cases, it is the only kind of evidence. The law presumes that testimony will be "admitted" unless there is a very good reason for the judge not to consider parts of it. But many cases involve other kinds of evidence—contracts, letters, email printouts, other documents, photographs, and objects. The law does not automatically admit these kinds of evidence. Before a judge can consider anything that is not testimony, a party must "offer" it into evidence. If the judge accepts the evidence, it becomes an **exhibit.**

How do you go about getting evidence admitted? Here's an example:

You went to an auto repair shop because your car had an oil leak; the owner told you your engine had a cracked head, and offered to rebuild the engine for $2500. You had the good sense to ask the mechanic to save all the discarded parts for you. (No shop has a duty to do that unless you ask.) You paid $2500 for the repair. When you went to visit your friend Cammie Shaft, a former mechanic, the following week, she saw the old head in the back seat of your car. She inspected the "cracked" head, and determined there was nothing wrong with it. You email the original shop and demand reimbursement of your $2500. The shop emails back to say it can't be responsible for everything that goes wrong on your old car.

Now, in court, you tell the judge: "I took my 1986 Chevy to Clunker's Auto Repair because of an oil leak on June 12, 2012. Paul Clunker, the owner, told me the head was cracked and that he would rebuild the engine for $2500. After the repair was made, another mechanic inspected the head and found out it wasn't cracked at all. Your Honor, I have here the original head and *I offer it into evidence*."

The judge will tell you to show the head to the defendant. The judge may tell the defendant he can object to this evidence. (More about that, below.) Once you have shown the part to the defendant, take it to the trial assistant and ask for it to be marked as an exhibit. Although a few courts won't assign a specific exhibit number, in most case the judge's assistant will give your exhibit a number (such as Plaintiff's Exhibit 1 or Defendant's Exhibit 101). Now the un-cracked head is admitted into evidence, and the judge is able to base his or her ruling on what the head looks like. When you get back to your table, write down the number assigned to the exhibit in case you need to refer to it again.

When it is the defendant's turn to talk, he says, "Your honor, I knew none of the facts that the plaintiff is talking about today. I never heard him complain about any problems. He's not dealing in good faith." When he finishes his defense, you ask the judge to allow you time for **rebuttal.** You say, "I emailed the defendant three days after I paid him for the unnecessary work—and he emailed this reply to me the following day. *I offer a printout of our emails into evidence to show defendant was aware of the problem*." After showing the printout to the defendant, you take the printout to the assistant for marking as an exhibit. The judge can now take into account that the defendant was lying.

Why does the opposing party get to object to exhibits?

Because a judge hears firsthand what the parties in a case have to say, the judge doesn't have to wonder if what he or she is hearing is the "real thing". But anyone can create a document or present other evidence that isn't the real thing; it's up to the other party to show that it's a fake. So, in every trial, the judge makes sure that the opposing party has a chance to examine the other side's proposed exhibits before accepting them into evidence.

Looking at the example above, imagine that you are not very honorable. When you offer the original head into evidence, Paul Clunker looks at it and says, "I object, Your Honor. This isn't the head from his Chevy—it's from a Saab. Look—right here it says, 'Made in Sweden'." The judge may want to see the head—but will not allow it into evidence as proof your Chevy didn't have a cracked head.

As for the printout of the emails, unless the defendant sees that the emails were sent to and from someone else that you wrongly say was the defendant, he will not be able to object to the admission of the emails as evidence. He doesn't want the judge to see the emails, because they contradict his testimony—but that's not a reason to object. *A party should object only if he or she has good reason to believe a piece of evidence isn't authentic.*

When a party in a case hands you a document or other item to examine before offering it to the judge as evidence, look at it. Carefully. Is the contract the other side wants the judge to consider the same as the contract you signed? If not, you must object or the court will accept it. Is that your signature on the check that a merchant says you bounced at her store? Is the check number even one in the sequence of checks you own? If not, object and say they are not authentic. Look at dates, signatures, page numbers, and other indicators of authenticity to make sure that what the judge will be looking at is accurate. Note that photocopies are as good as originals--unless they have been altered. If you are offering photographs or videos of a scene or event, you need to say whether they accurately depict the scene at the time of the event in question.

Testimony

Once you (and any witnesses you might have) are sworn in, statements you make about the facts of your case are under oath. Making false statements under oath is a felony; stick to facts you know to be true.

It's extremely important to describe clearly what your case is about. Remember: you are familiar with your case, but no one else is. It's also important to state facts, not opinions or conclusions. Here's an example of the difference:

FACTS	OPINIONS, CONCLUSIONS
I moved into the rental at 227 Forest Street, My City, on December 1, 2012.	I got suckered into renting this place at 227 Forest Street, My City, on December 1, 2012.
When I inspected the apartment, I pointed out to the landlord that there was mildew climbing the wall of the shower.	When I inspected this dump, I pointed out to this slumlord that the bathroom was full of mold and mildew.
The landlord said he would look into the problem and fix it. When I moved in the following week, there was still mildew in the bathroom.	The scumbag told me he'd look into the problem—the liar! When I moved in the following week, the bathroom hadn't been touched.

The shower floor was slippery from the mildew, and there was a strong odor of mold from the bathroom that I could smell from the rest of the apartment.

The place was disgusting!

I wrote a letter to the landlord on March 3, 2012 to insist that he fix the mold problem within 10 days. He did not fix it.

I wrote this sleazeball a letter telling him what he could do. He couldn't have cared less. He just wanted my money, the thief.

Instead, the landlord brought me a 30-day eviction notice—six days after I moved in. I decided to move before things got worse. It cost me $240 to have my things boxed and moved across town, and I lost two days of work to having to move and clean the place. I make $12 an hour, for a total of $192. In addition, the landlord's action, taken as soon as he got my letter, is retaliatory, so I am entitled to $(amount) in statutory damages

Then he decided to 'fix' me. It cost me a fortune to move out.

The judge's ruling

Oregon law says the duty of the judge is to "dispense justice promptly and economically between the litigants" and to "make such orders as the judge deems to be right, just and equitable for the disposition of the controversy." For some judges, that instruction means simply telling the parties which one will get a judgment against the other party. For others, the judge may briefly explain the law that he or she is relying on to come to a decision. Some judges even explain which facts they relied on, and describe how those facts influenced the decision.

If the plaintiff wins the case, the judge will want to know how much it cost to serve the defendant. That amount (cost of certified mail, payment to sheriff or other process server, publication in a newspaper, etc.) will be included in the amount of the judgment the plaintiff gets. Sometimes a visiting or pro tem judge will not know the amount of the filing fee each party paid, and will need to know that, too, as it is included in the judgment against the losing side. Be sure to have your information ready, so you can claim all you are owed.

Special considerations for those who got a waiver or deferral of their court filing fees

You may have filed your side of the case after getting your fees deferred. If your fees (or even part of your fees) were deferred rather than waived, your signed application became your promise to pay later. When you win your case, you will get a court judgment in your favor against the other party. The judge can add the balance of your deferred fees to the judgment against the other party. The other side will then owe you a certain amount based on your claim, and will owe the state (or the county, if the case is in justice court) the amount of the fees. Judges may not notice that your fees were deferred, however. If they don't, part of the court's judgment will include a judgment against you for the amount of any fee you still owe. This judgment can hurt your credit score. If you have good credit and want to protect it, here are two things you can do to prevent this problem:

1. After you file your complaint or answer to the complaint, pay off the deferred amount of the filing fee in full before the date of your hearing. If even a few dollars remain on this IOU to the court, that amount can be made into a judgment against you.
2. When the judge announces that you have won the case, ask the judge to make the other side the **judgment debtor** for the amount of your filing fee that remains unpaid. (Be sure to state the specific amount.) Oregon law allows the judge to do this. The losing side then has the responsibility of paying the deferred part of the fee; you are no longer responsible for paying it. There's no record to harm your credit.

If you obtained a filing fee deferral and lost your case, you will have two judgments against you—one with the other party as the judgment creditor and one with the state or county as judgment creditor. If you are able to make only small payments on those judgments, check with the court clerk about the interest rate and collection fees charged by the government on these accounts. If the cost of that "loan" from the government is significantly higher than the 9 per cent interest on the other judgment, you may want to make a special effort to take care of the debt to the court first.

Adding fees and interest to the judgment

In a contract dispute, the judge will want to know if the contract called for interest on the unpaid balance, and, if so, what amount of interest was due as of the day of the hearing. If you are the prevailing party, you must have that information ready. (If you're an Internet user, you can find free interest calculator websites.) The judge also may want to know the rate of interest the contract allowed.

The judge's decision

In cases that involve long written contracts or a large amount of other written material, or in cases with complicated legal issues, the judge may decide not to make a decision at the hearing. Instead, the judge will spend time reviewing the documents or researching the law, sending a decision in the mail later. If you move to a new address before you get the decision, be sure to alert the court clerk!

If the judge signs the judgment at the time of the hearing, the judge or the judge's assistant usually will tell the parties to go to the clerk's office to get copies of the judgment and record any payment made at that time. If you offer full or partial payment, get a receipt that states the amount and the date, and the court case number, signed by the other party. Keep it, to prevent problems later on.

It is the lucky prevailing party who gets full payment immediately after the judge has ruled. One study found that about 30% of prevailing parties get paid, and many must use formal collections procedures to do so. See Chapter 11, "Collecting Your Judgment."

Mediated settlements and stipulated judgments of dismissal

Courts in some counties offer mediation for people with small claims cases. In others, judges encourage people to work out their differences in the hallway and come back to report the results of their discussion. If the parties do come to an agreement (a **stipulation**), they should tell the judge what they agreed to. In almost all cases where the parties come up with a solution, the judge will agree to sign a judgment making the agreement official and enforceable.

The label the judgment has will be important to the person who lost the case. An ordinary court judgment gives the winner collection rights; it also hurts the losing party's credit because ordinary judgments get reported to national credit bureaux. A stipulated judgment has the same effect, unless it is a stipulated judgment of **dismissal**. A stipulated judgment of dismissal will not be reported as negative information to credit bureaux. This kind of judgment can be made contingent on the losing party—or both parties'—stipulating to do something in the future. If the party does not comply with the agreement by the deadline to which the parties stipulate, the other party can re-open the case and obtain the judgment he or she sought originally. In most Oregon counties, the prevailing party must file additional paperwork for which there are no standard forms and wait—sometimes for a fair bit of time—before getting a hearing. In a few counties, however, if a party does not follow the agreement, an SLR allows the other party to file an **affidavit of noncompliance**, and the court will enter a judgment against the person who did not follow the agreement. Example: Plaintiff sold defendant a defective ceiling fan for $400. Defendant stopped making payments for the fan after plaintiff refused to fix it. The balance on the bill is $200. Plaintiff sues defendant for $200 in Multnomah County small claims court. The parties settle the case by agreeing plaintiff will fix the fan, and defendant will pay $100. Plaintiff will accept $100 as full payment. If plaintiff makes the repair and defendant does not pay $100, plaintiff can file an affidavit for noncompliance, and the court will sign a judgment for $200, plus filing fees and costs and prevailing party fee, without another hearing. If plaintiff fixes the fan and then tries to charge the defendant $200 after agreeing to accept $100, the defendant can file an affidavit of noncompliance, and the court will sign a judgment denying the plaintiff the right to get any money from the defendant and giving the defendant the right to get court costs and a prevailing party fee from the plaintiff.

"I missed my trial!"

Small claims judges can set aside their decisions "for good cause shown" for up to 60 days after the original hearing date. What seems to be "good cause" for one judge may not be good cause for another, however. Still, it is safe to say that while almost all judges would consider the sudden death of a spouse or an unexpected hospitalization a good reason to miss a hearing, almost none would be sympathetic to an "I overslept" excuse.

If you miss your hearing and think you have a good reason to get another chance to have the case heard, send a letter to the court as soon as possible explaining the problem and asking the judge to set aside the judgment and re-set the case for a hearing. Be sure to say in your letter that you are sending a copy of it to the other side in your case—and send both letters at the same time. Keep a second copy for your own records.

Some judges will require a hearing to determine whether to set aside the judgment. If they agree your reason was good enough, some will want to have your trial immediately. Find out from the court clerk whether the judge intends to do that—if you need witnesses or evidence to put on your case, they will have to be there for the judge to be able to rule your way.

When the case is over—small claims in circuit court

In almost every court case, someone "wins" and someone "loses." In a few cases, a judge will decide that both parties were in the wrong, and neither will come away from court with anything but a foul mood. For people who haven't prevailed in a regular case in circuit court, there is a chance that the Oregon court of appeals can find a reason to change the result. If you've lost your case in the small claims department of the circuit court, however, you have no recourse. It's over. Still, if you learned something about the law and how to protect your legal rights in the process, you have gotten something of value from the experience.

Look at Chapter 11, "Collecting Your Judgment," to see what can happen next.

When the case is over—small claims in justice court

If your case turned out badly in a small claims hearing in a justice court, you may have the right to appeal the decision—depending on which party you are and on whether the defendant filed a counterclaim in the original case. Look at Chapter 12, "Appeals from Justice Court."

CHAPTER 11

Collecting the judgment

If you won your small claims case, you are now a **judgment creditor.** If you lost, you are a **judgment debtor.** What happens now?

If you are the judgment debtor, pay the debt if at all possible. If the judgment is for $10 or more, the judgment gives the judgment creditor the right to use certain procedures to collect money from you if you won't willingly or can't pay. The judgment also gives the creditor the right to collect 9 per cent simple interest on the unpaid balance of the debt starting from the day the judgment is entered into the court's record book. This interest amount might be different if the judgment is based on a case involving a contract that has a different interest amount. In that situation, most judges will order the contract interest amount as part of the judgment. If the judgment creditor uses any of the methods described in this chapter to collect the judgment debt, the creditor's cost for using it also is added to the original debt. These amounts add up fast.

If you are the judgment creditor, the judgment debtor may offer you full payment of the amount of the judgment or a smaller amount. If you get full payment right away, prepare a receipt for the debtor and file a **satisfaction of judgment** with the court clerk. (See a sample form at the end of this chapter.) If you are willing, under the principle of "a bird in the hand is worth two in the bush," to accept a smaller payment as payment in full, do the same thing. If the debtor does not offer immediate payment after the court decision, you must wait for two business days before you take any steps to collect. The small claims court clerk, meanwhile, will "enter" the judgment, making it official. Once the judgment is entered, you are authorized to use **garnishment** and **execution**, both described below. You may also want to put a **lien** on any real estate that the judgment debtor owns.

Note that, although you cannot normally use an attorney in small claims court, once you have a judgment you can hire a lawyer to help you collect it. Some lawyers will do specific things for a fixed fee; some will agree to accept a percentage of any amount you are able to collect. If the amount of the judgment is small, a lawyer's help (beyond a consultation) may not be worth the expense. Some judgment creditors sell their judgment to a collection agency for a percentage of the amount of the judgment; the collection agency then "owns" the debt and can keep anything it collects. If the judgment debtor later pays the judgment creditor, the creditor must notify the collection agency, which will want some or all of the payment.

Garnishing wages and accounts

The most common way to collect a judgment from a judgment debtor is **garnishment.** Garnishment allows a judgment creditor to draw some types of funds from the debtor's bank or credit union account. It can be used to order an employer to take a percentage of an employee's wages out of the employee's paycheck and to send the money to the creditor instead. It can be used in other situations in which the debtor is owed money by someone else, just as in the situation where an employer "owes" money to an employee for work done. For example, a landlord is owed money every month from the tenants who live in the rentals. A former tenant or anyone else who has a judgment against a landlord can garnish the rent payments to be made by current tenants—in short, intercepting the money that would otherwise go to the landlord.

Garnishment can be used to get payment from individuals or from businesses, usually from bank accounts. There are several other types of funds that a garnishment can capture, not discussed here. An attorney can describe those other sources, which are more difficult to access.

Executing on the judgment debtor's belongings

Executing on the judgment debtor's belongings works almost like garnishment—except that it requires the sheriff's department to do the taking. If you are trying to get payment from a business, the sheriff can perform a "till tap"—collecting money on hand at the business site, such as in the cash register at the garage of the auto mechanic who sold you that "new" battery or the coffee shop whose owner cheated you out of your wages. You must have the sheriff execute on the judgment in order to take property other than cash: cars, equipment, tools, Heisman trophies, gold records, etc. The sheriff holds an auction where the belongings go to the highest bidder. The amount the auction brings in could be lower or higher than the amount due under the judgment.

Depending on what the judgment creditor is trying to take, this method of collecting can be more difficult, both physically and legally: how do you remove a backhoe from someone's locked warehouse and get it to your place without a key or a tow truck? How do you get the title cleared out of the debtor's name and into your own name so you can sell it to pay off the debt? What do you have to do if the thing you attach is worth more than the amount of the debt? (Hint: You don't get to keep the difference.) What if the debtor still owes money to a third person who sold the vehicle to the debtor? What if someone else already has a lien on the vehicle? If you plan to take the debtor's belongings to pay off the judgment, you are likely to need help from a lawyer.

Protections for the judgment debtor

Fortunately for the judgment debtor, there are strict limits on what a non-government judgment creditor can take from you, so you won't be left naked and shivering in the Oregon rain. Some money and property are **exempt** from garnishment and attachment. Here's what a private judgment creditor cannot take, according to the law in 2018:

MONEY EXEMPT FROM GARNISHMENT

I. The larger of 75 per cent of a person's "disposable" earnings or this amount:
    a. $218 per week for someone paid weekly or more often
    b. $435 for someone paid bi-weekly

c. $468 for someone paid semi-monthly

d. $936 for someone paid monthly

Earnings include wages, salaries, commissions, bonuses, and other compensation. Disposable earnings are what is left after the deduction of amounts required to be withheld by law. The deducted amounts always include state and federal taxes, 401(k) contributions, Social Security, and Medicare. They include union dues if the debtor is a union member.

Example 1:

Disposable weekly earnings of judgment debtor	$400
75 per cent of disposable weekly earnings	$300
Amount that can be garnished from earnings (25 per cent of $400 is $100, an amount smaller than the difference between $218 and $400)	$100

Example 2:

Disposable weekly earnings of judgment debtor	$240
75 per cent of disposable weekly earnings	$180
Amount that can be garnished from earnings ($218 is larger than 75 per cent)	$44

Example 3:

Disposable weekly earnings of judgment debtor	$600
75 per cent of disposable weekly earnings	$450
Amount that can be garnished from earnings (75 per cent of $600 is larger than $218)	$150

What happens if a person's earnings are already being garnished by someone else, such as a child support enforcement agency or other judgment creditor? If the amount being garnished by someone else amounts to less than 75 per cent of the judgment debtor's disposable income and the balance of the income is higher than the amounts listed above, you will be able to garnish the difference between what the other creditor takes and the amount the debtor is allowed to keep. If the other creditor takes all of the earnings that can be garnished, you wait in line. You get nothing until that creditor has finished collecting his or her debt.

Example:

Other creditor is owed $125, week 1	
Disposable weekly earnings of judgment debtor	$400
75 per cent of disposable weekly earnings	$300
Amount other creditor can garnish	$100
Amount you can garnish	$0

After garnishing $100, other creditor is now owed $25, week 2

Disposable weekly earnings of judgment debtor	$400
75 per cent of disposable weekly earnings	$300
Garnishable amount	$100
Other creditor garnishes	$25
Amount you can garnish	$75

Even government creditors (such as the collectors of government-subsidized student loans, overdue taxes, and child support enforcement authorities) are limited in what they can take from debtors who are not acting in bad faith. The limits are higher than those described above that are imposed on private judgment creditors, and they always take priority over private creditors.

The following items are also exempt from garnishment:

II.   Spousal support (alimony), child support, or "separate maintenance" (support for someone who is legally separated but not divorced) reasonably necessary to support the debtor and his or her dependents. If you're trying to collect from these sources, you will probably need advice from, and representation by, a lawyer.

III.   Up to $10,000 (or property that can be traced back to it) in payment, or the right to that payment, compensating the debtor or the debtor's parent or legal guardian for a bodily injury.

IV.   Payment (or property than can be traced back to it), or the right to receive payment to compensate the debtor or the debtor's parent or legal guardian for the loss of future earnings; compensation for lost future earnings is often part of a personal injury settlement or award. This exemption is limited to the amount reasonably necessary for future support. If you're trying to collect from this source, you will likely need advice from, and possibly representation by, a lawyer.

V.   Veterans' benefits and loans.

VI. A federal earned income tax credit (EITC) or money that can be traced back to it, such as money from an EITC now in a bank account.

VII. Most income from public and private pensions, including Social Security.

VIII. Funds in a bank account from wages, retirement benefits, unemployment benefits, disability benefits, Social Security, Supplemental Security Income (SSI), or needs-based welfare benefits such as Temporary Assistance for Needy Families (TANF) or general assistance (GA). Except for Social Security and SSI, however, the exemption protects only the first $7,500.

IX. Unemployment benefits, TANF, and other public assistance not in a bank account.

X.   Proceeds from health insurance.

XI. Disability proceeds from life insurance.

XII. Cash surrender value of life insurance policies that are not payable to your estate.

XIII. Your right to receive payments under a crime victim reparation law, or property that you obtained by using reparation payments.

XIV. Prescribed health aids, such as walkers, wheelchairs, hospital beds, computer voice-recognition systems for anyone in the family.

XV. Federal annuities.

XVI. Other annuities, up to $250 per month. (Amount above that is treated like wages, above.)

THINGS EXEMPT FROM GARNISHMENT OR EXECUTION:

1. Household goods, furniture, radios, a TV set, and utensils with a total value of up to $3,000. Unless everything is brand new, the value is thrift-store value, not the original purchase price. Things you received as gifts count, even if you didn't pay anything for them.

2. A car, truck, trailer, or other vehicle worth up to $3,000. If the judgment debt is against more than one debtor, and any of those debtors are part owner of the vehicle, each person can claim the $3,000 exemption.

Thus, a married couple or domestic partners who both were sued can now claim a total of $6,000 as the exempt amount for a vehicle.

3. Tools, equipment, and other items needed for work, valued at up to $3,000. Again, more than one judgment debtor can claim this amount.

4. Books, pictures, and musical instruments worth up to $600 per debtor.

5. Clothing, jewelry, and personal items worth up to $1,800 per debtor.

6. Domestic animals and poultry for family use worth up to $1,000, along with 60 days' worth of food for the animals.

7. Food and fuel for the family for 60 days.

8. $400 in value of any personal property (not real estate), so long as it is not added to another exemption on the same property. If you have exempt belongings (see attachment exemption list, above), you can't add this $400 to the exemption value of that belonging. You can, however, apply the $400 exemption to the value of something that wouldn't otherwise be exempt.

9. A rifle or shotgun and a pistol, valued at up to $1,000 in total.

Another exemption, only for home owners, is called the homestead exemption. It protects up to $40,000 of the value of your home, or $50,000 if you own the home jointly with another judgment debtor. The home can be a house, a manufactured dwelling, or a floating home that you, your spouse, your parent, or your child occupies. If you have sold your home within the last year and intend to use the proceeds from the sale to buy another home before the year is out, the proceeds are exempt up to $40,000, or $50,000 if there are co-owners.

How does the garnishment process work? An order called a **writ** goes to a bank or an employer or business, called the **garnishee**. As the judgment creditor, you are now the **garnishor**. Under the writ, the garnishee must turn over any money it has in the name of the judgment debtor, up to the amount of the judgment debt. If the garnishee is a financial institution or a business, the writ requires it to turn over money for the next 45 days, up to the amount of the judgment debt. If the garnishee is an employer, the writ lasts for 90 days.

If you are able to get any money from the garnishment, you must hold it in the state for at least 10 days. The judgment debtor then has up to 120 days to file a **claim of exemption** in court, if he or she believes that you are not entitled to some or all of the money you have garnished because it is protected by Oregon's exemption law. In other words—don't spend the money until that time period is over, because you may have to give it back.

If the judgment debtor files this claim, the court will schedule a hearing to find out what, if anything, the creditor can keep. As soon as you receive notice of the hearing, you must turn the money over to the court until the hearing addresses the claim of exemption.

You can obtain garnishment forms from the court clerk where the judgment was entered or from an attorney. The packet contains seven different forms. The bank or employer or business gets:

- The original or a certified true copy of the writ of garnishment
- A garnishee response form
- Instructions to the garnishee
- A wage exemption calculation form.

The judgment debtor gets:

- A copy of the writ
- The original debt calculation form
- A list of exemptions
- A form to challenge the garnishment based on the exemptions

If you're the judgment debtor, you will be disappointed to know that the challenge to the garnishment does not allow you to dispute whether the debt is valid. The small claims court hearing was your only chance to do that. (You may be able to set aside a default judgment if you did not attend your trial; see Chapter 10.)

The garnishment documents for an employer garnishee can be personally delivered by an adult other than the judgment creditor, or they can be mailed by certified mail (return receipt requested). Many creditors use the sheriff's office for this service, for which there is a fee. The documents for the debtor must be delivered or mailed on the same date.

When the garnishor is looking for a bank account, it is common to have the writ delivered to the bank or credit union in person and the copy and other documents sent by certified mail to the debtor. That way, the debtor will not be able to remove money from the bank before the writ takes effect. Only a sheriff's department or a professional server with "errors and omissions" insurance can do in-person delivery; your cousin or your friend can't help you here. When a writ of garnishment goes to a financial institution, it is effective for every account at every branch in the state.

For the judgment debtor, this method of serving the writ can mean that he or she bounces checks unknowingly—not only losing the money in the account but also accruing NSF check fees. If you are concerned that your account may be garnished, verify that you have enough money in it to cover any checks as you write them. Some people close their accounts to avoid this extra cost.

A possible problem for the creditor arises if the creditor doesn't know the correct name of the debtor. A garnishee bank will not honor a writ if it is not certain whether the writ applies to one of its customers. Another possible issue arises when the forms are not filled out correctly and completely, in that the sheriff will not serve a defective writ. Finally, the judgment creditor must be sure to include payment to the bank of $15 for each debtor or the bank will not have to honor the writ. The payment to the bank can be added to the amount of the judgment debt. A writ of garnishment to an employer or a business does not require this payment.

The judgment creditor can obtain a new writ of garnishment after 45 days (financial institutions and businesses) or 90 days (employers), and can keep doing so until the debt is paid off.

How does the execution process work? Instead of a writ of garnishment, a **writ of execution** is the document you will want the court clerk to issue. In this case, the writ goes to a sheriff in the county where the things are. The writ must have detailed information: which things to take for sale, where they are, and the names and last known addresses of the debtor and anyone else entitled to notice. There is a fee for this service, which can sometimes be substantial. The civil process department of the sheriff's office can provide information about the sale process, and give you an estimate of the cost. The sheriff's office will require you to post a bond to cover any losses it incurs, too.

As you can see, the process itself can be complicated, especially if the debtor claims that some of the property is exempt. Getting a lawyer's help is a very good idea if you pursue this option.

Finding out what the debtor owns and where it is

For the judgment creditor, it's helpful to do some basic investigation before going to the trouble of going after money and assets. If you have done business with the judgment debtor, you may have accepted checks; that means you can see where the debtor has (or had) at least one bank account. If the debtor lives in the area, you or a friend can drive by the debtor's home. If the debtor lives in an apartment, you won't be looking at a homestead exemption.

If the debtor lives in a house or in what might be condominiums, check with a title company or the county assessor's office to see who owns the property. You can also ask if the debtor owns real estate elsewhere. How many cars are at the home, and what are their make, model, and age? Take down license plate numbers. If you drive past at night, you may get to see that 58-inch television set in the living room, across from those elegant leather couches. But stay off the property!

You can ask neighbors what they know about the debtor, but be careful. First, they are likely to tell the debtor someone was asking; second, you shouldn't disclose that the debtor owes you money or that you seek information to help you to collect. State and federal debt collection laws in many cases prohibit your broadcasting that someone owes you money on certain kinds of debts.

If the debtor operates a business, visit the business site or sites, both when the business is open and when it is closed. Are there company vehicles? Is there equipment? How many cars are parked in the company lot? These items may be available for execution if the debtor is the business or if the business belongs to the debtor.

Visit any court clerk's office or a law library, where staff can help you look online to see records of all published Oregon court cases involving the judgment debtor on the Oregon Case Judicial Information Network (OCJIN). This information can sometimes alert you to other property, the debtor's marital status and criminal history, and show you if there are other cases in which this person is a judgment debtor.

Judgment debtor exam

If you are the judgment creditor, the activities outlined above may provide you with all the information you need to be able to garnish the judgment creditor's bank accounts, business cash registers, or wages and commissions. If not, you can get a court order for a **judgment debtor examination.** A debtor's examination, also called a debtor's appearance, requires the debtor to appear in court, take an oath, and then answer your questions about bank and other accounts, stocks, bonds, other investments, real estate, and personal property.

You must file a motion and an affidavit seeking this kind of order. See Appendix B for some sources of sample documents for this purpose.

You can use this remedy only after you (1) have been unsuccessful in using garnishment or attachment (or both) in getting full payment of the judgment debt or (2) can prove that you sent a written demand for payment of the judgment (proof such as a certified mail receipt).

The court order can ask the debtor to bring certain documents. In some cases, it can include a restraining order to keep the debtor from hiding or getting rid of property. The judgment creditor can subpoena witnesses to talk about the debtor's finances and assets, too—spouses, former spouses, accountants, etc.

The order should go to the debtor by personal service by someone other than the judgment creditor, along with a copy of the motion and affidavit. If the debtor does not appear for the examination, the creditor can file a **motion to show cause** (give a reason) for not appearing. The court will sign an order setting a hearing where the debtor can explain. A copy of this order must be personally served on the debtor. If the debtor ignores this order, he or she can be held in contempt of court and subject to fines. In some cases, the judgment debtor may even be arrested.

If you are the judgment debtor, do not ignore the debtor examination notice. Attend the examination, taking all requested documents with you. But leave most of your cash at home because one question that the judgment creditor can ask you is, "How much money do you have with you right now?"—and take it. You don't want to have to go through the claim of exemption process, especially when it will be difficult to show that the cash is exempt.

If you turn over money or other things of value at a debtor's examination or any other time, insist on getting a receipt from the judgment creditor. Everything you pay should be subtracted from the amount of the judgment against you. The judgment creditor has a duty to file a form called a **partial satisfaction of judgment** every time you pay down the debt, and a **full satisfaction of judgment** once the debt is paid off. To protect your rights, send a letter to the court clerk with a copy of the receipt every time you get one. Keep copies for yourself, too, and keep those receipts until the judgment creditor submits a full satisfaction of judgment.

Check with the court clerk a week to 10 days later to see if the judgment creditor has filed a satisfaction. If that hasn't happened, you may want to fill in a satisfaction form yourself and get the creditor to sign it. If the judgment creditor won't cooperate, you can submit proof of payment to the court yourself. In a few cases, you will have to file a motion with the court to require the creditor to acknowledge your payment.

If you are the judgment creditor, make sure you file satisfactions promptly. For some kinds of debts, creditors may be subject to penalties under the federal Fair Credit Reporting Act if they do not report changes in the amount of the judgment to the court.

Lien on real estate

A judgment creditor can put a lien on a judgment debtor's real property (land and buildings). What does a lien on the judgment debtor's real estate do? When real estate has a lien on it, the owner can't sell the property without paying off the lien. It may be years before the land goes up for sale, but when it does, you will get your money if you haven't collected it already—and if your judgment is still enforceable.

Important: Almost all kinds of judgments in Oregon are enforceable for 10 years. If you haven't been able to collect your money within that time period, you have the right to renew the judgment for another 10 years. You must renew it *before* it expires, by filing a "certificate of extension."

Here's how to put a lien on the judgment debtor's real property: If you obtained your judgment in the small claims department of circuit court, you must **transcribe** the judgment to circuit court, turning the small claims judgment into a circuit court judgment. There is a small fee—around $15--to do this; contact the court clerk for instructions. Keep a receipt for this expense and any other expenses that you incur trying to collect the debt. These costs can be added to the amount of the judgment later on.

When the judgment is transcribed, it becomes a lien on any real estate that the judgment debtor owns—or might own in the future--in the county where you got the judgment. If you know that the debtor owns property in other counties in the state, you can create a judgment lien in those counties, too. There is a small fee for that service. Some title companies will be willing to let you know where else the debtor has real estate.

To create a judgment lien in another county, you can send to the county clerk in that other county (the clerk in the recorder's office, not the court clerk) a **certified** copy of the judgment or a **lien record abstract.** If you plan to send a certified copy of the judgment, find out from the county clerk what the county's rules are regarding page margins and any information needed on the first page of the document. If the certified copy doesn't look the way the county clerk wants it, the clerk will not file the document. To avoid the problem, just put a cover sheet on the judgment that has the right margins and information.

If you obtained your judgment from a justice court, you can have the judgment transcribed or simply file a certified copy of the justice court judgment or a lien abstract record with the county clerk's office where you got the judgment. You can record liens in other counties as described above.

In a few cases, a judgment creditor can **execute** on the real estate to get payment for the amount of the lien. The process is limited to judgments liens of more than $3,000 (not counting interest, court costs, and prevailing party fees). If there is a mortgage on the property, tax liens, or other judgment liens

154

already on the property, you would have to pay off all of those liens, as well as the amount of any homestead exemption, before being able to take title to the property. The process is complicated and expensive, and not to be done without assistance from a lawyer. Executing on real estate subject to a judgment lien is rarely the right move for the amount of a judgment in small claims court. If you are able to recover some or all of what is owed you through this process, however, remember to file a satisfaction of judgment form with the court.

Judgment liens on real estate sometimes don't get paid off when the property changes hands. In some cases, the owner gives the property to other family members or friends, or may sell whatever rights the owner has in the property via a "quit claim" deed. Those don't make your lien go away, but because there is no mortgage or title company involved, there is no pressure on the seller or buyer to clear the lien from the property. Another situation that could prevent your collecting is a foreclosure on the property by a mortgage lender. A foreclosure will wipe out your lien.

There's one more way a judgment lien on real estate can be made unenforceable: the debtor declares bankruptcy and gets the debt discharged (canceled). The debtor could file for bankruptcy at any time, actually; if you get a notice from the bankruptcy court or if you find out some other way that the debtor has filed for bankruptcy, *do not continue with your case* unless and until the bankruptcy is over and your claim was not discharged by the bankruptcy. See a bankruptcy lawyer for more information about your rights and duties.

SAMPLE satisfaction of judgment form

IN THE CIRCUIT COURT OF THE STATE OF OREGON
FOR THE COUNTY OF WASHINGTON
SMALL CLAIMS DEPARTMENT

Paul Plaintiff,
      plaintiff

vs

Dan Defendant,
      defendant.

FULL OR PARTIAL
SATISFACTION OF JUDGMENT

Case no. SC 13-81627

Received $170.00 this 17th day of September, 2017, in partial satisfaction of judgment in the above-entitled Court and Cause.

Paul Plaintiff
_____
Judgment Creditor

SUBSCRIBED and sworn before me this 17th day of September, 2017.

Alicia Administrator
_____
Trial court administrator/Clerk/Notary

My commission expires May 18, 2019

CHAPTER 12

Appealing your case to circuit court

Throughout this book, you've seen references to procedures in small claims courts that are part of a circuit court and small claims procedures in justice courts. Although there are many similarities between the two types of courts, there are also some important differences.

One significant difference is that the person who decides the case in justice court is a justice of the peace rather than a judge. A justice of the peace is not required to be a lawyer but any non-lawyer justice of the peace must attend at least 30 hours of law-related training every two years. So you might not get the level of legal expertise from a justice of the peace that you would usually find in a circuit court judge.

Another difference is that you may have the right, although it is limited, to appeal the decision of the justice of the peace. If you were the plaintiff in the small claims case, only the defendant has the right to appeal a decision in your favor. If the defendant won a counterclaim, only you, the plaintiff, can appeal the court's decision on the counterclaim. As you can see, it is possible for both sides to appeal if each side lost on a claim of the other.

The appeal goes to the circuit court, where you can make your case all over again. Because this circuit court appearance is an appeal, you are not entitled to a jury. Nor can you raise new claims beyond those you made in justice court, although you can increase the amount of the damages or restitution you asked for in small claims court—assuming you can justify it. You are allowed to get help from an attorney in the appeal. Depending on the kind of case it is, the attorney may be able to get his or her attorney fees paid by the other side if you win the case.

See Appendix C for a list of the counties in which justice court is the forum for small claims cases.

A party entitled to appeal from a justice court small claims decision has only ten days after the small claims judgment is entered in which to appeal to the circuit court in the same county. The judgment debtor is now an **appellant.** There is a standard form for the appeal, set out in ORS 55.120. The appellant must pay a new filing fee (approximately $200); in most cases, he or she also must post a **bond**. The small claims court **judgment creditor** becomes an **appellee,** who also has to pay a new filing fee of the same amount. Either side can seek a fee deferral or waiver if necessary.

What's a bond? It's a type of guarantee that you will do something. You have probably heard of bail bonds, which are a good example of how bonds work. Criminal defendants enter into a contract with a bail bondsman in which they promise to show up at their trials. They pay the bondsman to give the court a percentage of the bail amount ordered by the judge. If, later on, they show up for trial, the bondsman gets the money back. If they don't, the bondsman must pay the court the full amount of the bail.

Oregon doesn't have a bail bond industry, so you will have to try to get a bond through an insurance agent. The cost is a percentage of the estimated costs of the existing judgment against you, plus costs, fees, and attorney fees for the other party if that party were to win the appeal. Sometimes the insurer will want collateral, such as a claim to a house or a car or other valuables, to protect its investment.

There are alternatives to getting a bond. One is to deposit with the court the amount of cash that you estimate would cover the existing judgment and costs described above. Another, for someone who has little or no income or resources, is to ask for a waiver of the bond requirement "for good cause." The good cause, of course, is that, without any money, you are shut out of the courts unless the court waives the bond requirement. If you cannot afford the bond or a cash deposit and the court will not let you waive or defer the fees, seek legal advice quickly.

If you win your case on appeal to circuit court, you will get back any cash you paid into court, plus a prevailing party fee. The other party will no longer have a judgment against you. There is no further appeal.

APPENDIX A — SELECTED STATUTES

Chapter 46—Small Claims Department of Circuit Court

2017 EDITION

46.405 Small claims department; jurisdiction. (1) Except as provided in subsection (6) of this section, each circuit court shall have a small claims department.

(2) Except as provided in this section, all actions for the recovery of money, damages, specific personal property, or any penalty or forfeiture must be commenced and prosecuted in the small claims department if the amount or value claimed in the action does not exceed $750.

(3) Except as provided in this section, an action for the recovery of money, damages, specific personal property, or any penalty or forfeiture may be commenced and prosecuted in the small claims department if the amount or value claimed in the action does not exceed $10,000.

(4)(a) Class actions may not be commenced and prosecuted in the small claims department.

(b) An action by an inmate, as defined in ORS 30.642, against another inmate may not be commenced and prosecuted in the small claims department.

(5) Actions providing for statutory attorney fees in which the amount or value claimed does not exceed $750 may be commenced and prosecuted in the small claims department or may be commenced and prosecuted in the regular department of the circuit court. This subsection does not apply to an action based on contract for which attorney fees are authorized under ORS 20.082.

(6) If a circuit court is located in the same city as a justice court, the circuit court need not have a small claims department if the circuit court and the justice court enter into an intergovernmental agreement that provides that only the justice

161

court will operate a small claims department. If an intergovernmental agreement is entered into under this subsection, the agreement must establish appropriate procedures for referring small claims cases to the justice court. [1971 c.760 §2; 1973 c.812 §2; 1975 c.592 §1; 1979 c.567 §1; 1983 c.242 §1; 1985 c.367 §1; 1987 c.725 §1; 1995 c.227 §1; 1995 c.658 §43; 1997 c.378 §1; amendments by 1997 c.378 §2 repealed by 1999 c.84 §9; 1997 c.801 §78; 1999 c.84 §1; 1999 c.673 §1; 2001 c.542 §5; 2007 c.125 §1; 2011 c.262 §4; 2011 c.595 §47]

46.415 Circuit judges to sit in department; procedure. (1) The judges of a circuit court shall sit as judges of the small claims department.

(2) No formal pleadings other than the claim shall be necessary.

(3) The hearing and disposition of all cases shall be informal, the sole object being to dispense justice promptly and economically between the litigants. The parties shall have the privilege of offering evidence and testimony of witnesses at the hearing. The judge may informally consult witnesses or otherwise investigate the controversy and give judgment or make such orders as the judge deems to be right, just and equitable for the disposition of the controversy.

(4) No attorney at law or person other than the plaintiff and defendant and their witnesses shall appear on behalf of any party in litigation in the small claims department without the consent of the judge of the court.

(5) Notwithstanding the provisions of ORS 9.320, a corporation, the state or any city, county, district or other political subdivision or public corporation in this state, without appearance by attorney, may appear as a party to any action in the small claims department and in any supplementary proceeding in aid of execution after entry of a small claims judgment.

(6) Assigned claims may be prosecuted by an assignee in small claims department to the same extent they may be prosecuted in any other state court. [1971 c.760 §3; 1973 c.484 §6; 1981 s.s. c.1 §22; 1987 c.811 §1; 1993 c.282 §2; 1995 c.658 §44; 1997 c.808 §§6,7, 2015 c.7 §3]

46.425 Commencement of actions; contents of claim. (1) An action in the small claims department shall be commenced by the plaintiff's filing with the clerk of the court a claim in the form prescribed by the court.

(2) The claim shall contain the name and address of the plaintiff and of the defendant, followed by a plain and simple statement of the claim, including the amount and the date the claim allegedly accrued. The claim shall include an

affidavit signed by the plaintiff and stating that the plaintiff made a bona fide effort to collect the claim from the defendant before filing the claim with the clerk.

(3) Except in actions arising under ORS chapter 90, the plaintiff must include in a claim all amounts claimed from the defendant arising out of a single transaction or occurrence. Any plaintiff alleging damages on a transaction requiring installment payments need only claim the installment payments due and owing as of the date of filing of the claim, and need not accelerate the remaining payments. The plaintiff may include in a claim all amounts claimed from a defendant on more than one transaction or occurrence if the total amount of the claim does not exceed $10,000.

(4) Notwithstanding subsection (3) of this section, a plaintiff bringing an action on assigned claims:

(a) Need bring an action only on those claims that have been assigned as of the date the action is filed; and

(b) May bring separate actions for each person assigning claims to the plaintiff. [1971 c.760 §4; 1977 c.875 §2; 1991 c.195 §1; 1995 c.658 §45; 1997 c.378 §4; amendments by 1997 c.378 §5 repealed by 1999 c.84 §9; 1997 c.801 §80; 1999 c.84 §2; 2007 c.125 §2; 2011 c.595 §48, 2015 c. 121 §1]

46.441 Explanation to plaintiff of how notice may be served. The small claims department of a circuit court shall provide to each plaintiff who files a claim with the department a written explanation of how notice may be served in actions in the department. [1977 c.875 §9; 1995 c.658 §46]

46.445 Notice of claim; content; service. (1) Upon the filing of a claim in the small claims department of a circuit court, the clerk shall issue a notice in the form prescribed by the court.

(2) The notice shall be directed to the defendant, naming the defendant, and shall contain a copy of the claim.

(3) The notice and claim shall be served upon the defendant either in the manner provided for the service of summons and complaint in proceedings in the circuit courts or by certified mail, at the option of the plaintiff. If service by certified mail is attempted, the plaintiff shall mail the notice and claim by certified mail addressed to the defendant at the last-known mailing address of the defendant. The envelope shall be marked with the words "Deliver to Addressee Only" and "Return Receipt Requested." The date of delivery

appearing on the return receipt shall be prima facie evidence of the date on which the notice and claim was served upon the defendant. If service by certified mail is not successfully accomplished, the notice and claim shall be served in the manner provided for the service of summons and complaint in proceedings in the circuit courts.

(4) The notice shall include a statement in substantially the following form:

NOTICE TO DEFENDANT:
READ THESE PAPERS CAREFULLY!!

Within 14 DAYS after receiving this notice you MUST do ONE of the following things:

Pay the claim plus filing fees and service expenses paid by plaintiff OR Demand a hearing OR Demand a jury trial

If you fail to do one of the above things within 14 DAYS after receiving this notice, then upon written request from the plaintiff the clerk of the court will enter a judgment against you for the amount claimed plus filing fees and service expenses paid by the plaintiff, plus a prevailing party fee.

If you have questions about the small claims court filing procedures after reading this notice, you may contact the clerk of the court; however, the clerk cannot give you legal advice on the claim. [1971 c.760 §6; 1977 c.875 §4; 1977 c.877 §9a; 1989 c.741 §1; 1991 c.111 §4; 1991 c.195 §2; 1995 c.658 §47; 1997 c.872 §§8,9]

46.455 Admission or denial of claim; request for jury trial. Within 14 days after the date of service of the notice and claim upon the defendant as provided in ORS 46.445:

(1) If the defendant admits the claim, the defendant may settle it by:

(a) Paying to the plaintiff the amount of the claim plus the amount of all filing fees and service expenses paid by the plaintiff and mailing proof of that payment to the court.

(b) If the claim is for recovery of specific personal property, delivering the property to the plaintiff and paying to the plaintiff the amount of all filing fees and service expenses paid by the plaintiff and mailing proof of that delivery and payment to the court.

(2) If the defendant denies the claim, the defendant:

(a) May demand a hearing in the small claims department in a written request to the clerk in the form prescribed by the court, accompanied by payment of the defendant's fee prescribed; and

(b) When demanding a hearing, may assert a counterclaim in the form provided by the court.

(3) If the amount or value claimed exceeds $750, the defendant has a constitutional right to a jury trial and may claim that right in a written request to the clerk in the form prescribed by the court, accompanied by payment of the appearance fee required from defendants under ORS 21.160. The request shall designate a mailing address to which a summons and copy of the complaint may be served by mail. Thereafter, the plaintiff's claim will not be limited to the amount stated in the claim, though it must involve the same controversy. [1971 c.760 §7; 1973 c.654 §1; 1973 c.812 §3a; 1977 c.875 §5; 1977 c.877 §10a; 1981 s.s. c.3 §94; 1983 c.673 §2; 1985 c.496 §13; 1991 c.111 §5; 1991 c.195 §3; 1995 c.227 §2; 1995 c.455 §4; 1995 c.658 §48; 1997 c.46 §§6,7; 2011 c.595 §49]

46.461 Counterclaims; fee; transfer of case to circuit court. (1) The defendant in an action in the small claims department may assert as a counterclaim any claim that, on the date of issuance of notice pursuant to ORS 46.445, the defendant may have against the plaintiff and that arises out of the same transaction or occurrence that is the subject matter of the claim filed by the plaintiff.

(2) If the amount or value of the counterclaim exceeds $10,000, the court shall strike the counterclaim and proceed to hear and dispose of the case as though the counterclaim had not been asserted unless the defendant files with the counterclaim a motion requesting that the case be transferred from the small claims department to the circuit court. After the transfer the plaintiff's claim will not be limited to the amount stated in the claim filed with the small claims department, though it must involve the same controversy.

(3)(a) If the amount or value of the counterclaim exceeds that specified in subsection (2) of this section, and the defendant files a motion requesting transfer as provided in subsection (2) of this section, the case shall be transferred to the circuit court. The clerk of the court shall notify the plaintiff and defendant, by mail, of the transfer. The notice to the plaintiff shall contain a copy of the counterclaim and shall instruct the plaintiff to file with the court and serve by mail on the defendant, within 20 days following the mailing of the notice, a reply to the counterclaim and, if the plaintiff proposes to increase the amount of the claim originally filed with the small claims department, an amended claim for the increased amount. Proof of service on the defendant of the plaintiff's reply and amended claim may be made by certificate of the plaintiff or plaintiff's attorney attached to the reply and amended claim filed with the court. The defendant is not required to answer an amended claim of the plaintiff.

(b) Upon filing the motion requesting transfer, the defendant shall pay to the clerk of the court an amount equal to the difference between the fee paid by the defendant as required by ORS 46.570 and the fee required of a defendant under ORS 21.160. Upon filing a reply to the counterclaim, the plaintiff shall pay to the clerk of the court an amount equal to the difference between the fee paid by the plaintiff as required by ORS 46.570 and the fee required of a plaintiff under ORS 21.160. [1977 c.875 §10; 1979 c.567 §3; 1983 c.242 §2; 1983 c.673 §5; 1985 c.367 §2; 1985 c.496 §31; 1987 c.714 §9; 1987 c.725 §2; 1991 c.790 §7; 1995 c.658 §49; 1997 c.378 §7; amendments by 1997 c.378 §8 repealed by 1999 c.84 §9; 1997 c.801 §82; 1999 c.84 §3; 2007 c.125 §3; 2011 c.595 §50]

46.465 Time and place of hearing; notice; procedure if right to jury trial asserted; attorney fees. (1) If the defendant demands a hearing in the small claims department, under the direction of the court the clerk shall fix a day and time for the hearing and shall mail to the parties a notice of the hearing time in the form prescribed by the court, instructing them to bring witnesses, documents and other evidence pertinent to the controversy.

(2) If the defendant asserts a counterclaim, the notice of the hearing time shall contain a copy of the counterclaim.

(3)(a) If the defendant claims the right to a jury trial, the clerk shall notify the plaintiff by mail of the requirements of this paragraph. Within 20 days after the mailing of the notice, the plaintiff must file a formal complaint with the court and serve by mail a summons and copy of the complaint on the defendant at the designated address of the defendant. Proof of service must be filed by the plaintiff with the court. Proof of service may be made by filing a certificate of the plaintiff or the plaintiff's attorney with the complaint.

(b) The plaintiff's claim in the formal complaint filed pursuant to this subsection is not limited to the amount stated in the claim filed in the small claims department, but the claim in the formal complaint must relate to the same controversy.

(c) The defendant must file an appearance in the matter within 10 days after the date on which the summons and copy of the complaint would be delivered to the defendant in due course of mail. Thereafter the cause shall proceed as other causes in the court, and costs and disbursements shall be allowed and taxed. Fees not previously paid shall be charged and collected as provided for other cases tried in the circuit court, except that the filing fee for the plaintiff shall be an amount equal to the difference between the filing fee paid by the plaintiff as required by ORS 46.570 and the filing fee required of the plaintiff under ORS 21.160.

(4)(a) If the defendant claims the right to a jury trial and does not prevail in the action, the court shall award to the plaintiff reasonable attorney fees incurred by the plaintiff in the action. Unless attorney fees are otherwise provided for in the action by contract or statutory provision, attorney fees awarded under this paragraph may not exceed $1,000.

(b) If the defendant asserts a counterclaim that requires transfer of the matter under the provisions of ORS 46.461, and the defendant does not prevail in the action, the court shall award to the plaintiff reasonable attorney fees incurred by the plaintiff in the action. [1971 c.760 §8; 1975 c.346 §1; 1983 c.673 §3; 1985 c.496 §14; 1991 c.790 §8; 1995 c.455 §5; 1995 c.618 §15a; 1997 c.46 §§9,10; 2011 c.595 §51]

46.475 Additional time for appearances; default and dismissal. (1) Upon written request, the court may extend to the parties additional time within which to make formal appearances required in the small claims department of a circuit court.

(2) If the defendant fails to pay the claim, demand a hearing, or demand a jury trial and comply with ORS 46.465 (3)(c), upon written request from the plaintiff the clerk shall enter a judgment against the defendant for the relief claimed plus the amount of the small claims filing fees and service expenses paid by the plaintiff and the prevailing party fee provided by ORS 20.190.

(3) If the plaintiff fails within the time provided to file a formal complaint pursuant to ORS 46.465 (3)(a), the clerk shall dismiss the case without prejudice.

(4) If the defendant appears at the time set for hearing but no appearance is made by the plaintiff, the claim shall be dismissed with prejudice. If neither party appears, the claim shall be dismissed without prejudice.

(5) Upon good cause shown within 60 days, the court may set aside a default judgment or dismissal and reset the claim for hearing. [1971 c.760 §9; 1977 c.875 §6; 1985 c.496 §15; 1991 c.111 §6; 1995 c.618 §§8,8a; 1995 c.658 §51; 1997 c.46 §§12,13; 1999 c.84 §10; 2011 c.595 §52]

46.485 Extent and effect of small claims judgment. (1) In addition to any other award, the prevailing party shall be entitled to a judgment for the small claims filing fees and service expenses paid by the party and the prevailing party fee provided for in ORS 20.190 (1)(c) or (2)(b). The prevailing party may also be awarded prevailing party fees under ORS 20.190 (3). The award shall be paid or the property delivered upon such terms and conditions as the judge may prescribe.

(2) The court may allow to the defendant a setoff not to exceed the amount of plaintiff's claim, but in such case the court shall cause to be entered in the record the amount of the setoff allowed.

(3) No attachment shall issue on any cause in the small claims department.

(4) A judgment in the small claims department is conclusive upon the parties and no appeal may be taken from the judgment.

(5) The clerk of the court shall keep a record of all actions, proceedings and judgments in the small claims department.

(6) A judgment in the small claims department is a judgment of the circuit court. The clerk shall enter such judgment in the register of the circuit court in the manner provided by ORS 18.075. A judgment in the small claims department may create a lien as provided by ORS 46.488. Judgments that include money awards, as defined by ORS 18.005, are subject to ORS 18.042. [1971 c.760 §10; 1977 c.875 §7; 1985 c.540 §17; 1991 c.111 §7; 1995 c.618 §9; 1995 c.658 §52; 1997 c.801 §60; 1999 c.84 §8; 2003 c.576 §91]

46.488 Lien effect of small claims judgments. (1) A judgment creditor may not create a judgment lien for a judgment entered in the small claims department of a circuit court if the money award is less than $10, exclusive of costs and disbursements. A judgment creditor may create a judgment lien for a judgment entered in the small claims department of a circuit court in an amount of $10 or more and less than $3,000, exclusive of costs and disbursements, only as provided in subsection (3) of this section.

(2) If a judgment is rendered in the small claims department in an amount of $3,000 or more, the clerk shall note in the register of the circuit court that the judgment creates a judgment lien if the judgment otherwise complies with the requirements of ORS chapter 18 for creating a judgment lien. A judgment creditor may create a lien for the judgment in other counties in the manner provided by ORS 18.152.

(3) When a judgment is entered in the small claims department in an amount of $10 or more and less than $3,000, exclusive of costs or disbursements, a judgment creditor may at any time before expiration of judgment remedies for the judgment under ORS 18.180 create a judgment lien for the judgment by paying to the clerk of the court that entered the judgment the fees established under ORS 21.235 (1)(a) and requesting that the clerk of the court note in the register and in the judgment lien record that the judgment creates a judgment lien. Upon receipt of the fees and request for creating a judgment lien, the clerk shall note in the register that the judgment creates a judgment lien. Upon entry of the notation in the register, the judgment creates a lien as described in ORS 18.150, and a judgment creditor may create a lien for the judgment in other counties in the manner provided by ORS 18.152. [1997 c.801 §57; 1997 c.801 §58; 1999 c.195 §3; 1999 c.1095 §12; 2003 c.576 §92; 2003 c.737 §§77,78; 2007 c.339 §11; 2011 c.595 §119]

Note: Section 8 (1) and (2), chapter 195, Oregon Laws 1999, provides:

Sec. 8. (1) The amendments to ORS 18.350 by section 1 of this 1999 Act, and the amendments to ORS 46.488 by section 58, chapter 801, Oregon Laws 1997, and by section 3 of this 1999 Act, do not affect any judgment docketed in the circuit court under the provisions of ORS 46.488 (1997 Edition) before the effective date of this 1999 Act [October 23, 1999]. Notwithstanding the amendments to ORS 46.488 by section 58, chapter 801, Oregon Laws 1997, and by section 3 of this 1999 Act, any judgment entered in the small claims department of a circuit court before the effective date of this 1999 Act that was not docketed in the circuit court under the provisions of ORS 46.488 (1997 Edition) before the effective date of this 1999 Act may become a lien on real property only in the manner provided by ORS 46.488 (1997 Edition).

(2) Any judgment docketed before the effective date of this 1999 Act, including judgments docketed under the provisions of ORS 46.488 (1997

Edition), that did not become a lien on real property by reason of failure of the judgment creditor to file a lien certificate with the court in the manner required by ORS 18.350 (4) to (9) (1997 Edition) shall automatically become a lien on real property to the extent described in ORS 18.350, as amended by section 1 of this 1999 Act, on January 1, 2000, and shall be considered in all respects as though the judgment had been docketed on January 1, 2000. [1999 c.195 §8(1),(2); 1999 c.195 §8a(1),(2)]

46.560 Where action to be commenced and tried. (1) Except as provided in subsections (2) and (3) of this section, all actions in small claims department shall be commenced and tried in the county in which the defendants, or one of them, reside or may be found at the commencement of the action.

(2) When an action is founded on an alleged tort, it may be commenced either in the county where the cause of action arose or in the county where the defendants, or one of them, reside or may be found at the commencement of the action.

(3) When the defendant has contracted to perform an obligation in a particular county, action may be commenced in either that county or where the defendants, or one of them, reside or may be found at the commencement of the action. [1973 c.446 §2, 2015 c. 27§3]

46.570 Fees. The small claims department of a circuit court shall collect the following filing fees from the plaintiff when a claim is filed in the court, and from the defendant when the defendant demands a hearing:

(1) $53, when the amount claimed is $2,500 or less; and

(2) $95, when the amount is more than $2,500. [Formerly 46.221; 2003 c.737 §§44,45a,45c; 2005 c.702 §§49,50,51; 2007 c.129 §20; 2007 c.860 §7; 2011 c.595 §46; 2013 c.685 §§ 36, 36a; 2014 c.76 §10]

Chapter 55—Justice Court Small Claims Department

2017 EDITION

55.011 Small claims department; jurisdiction. (1) Except as provided in subsection (8) of this section, in each justice court created under any law of this state there shall be a small claims department.

(2) Except as provided in this section, all actions for the recovery of money, damages, specific personal property, or any penalty or forfeiture must be commenced and prosecuted in the small claims department if the amount or value claimed in the action does not exceed $750.

(3) Except as provided in this section, an action for the recovery of money, damages, specific personal property, or any penalty or forfeiture may be commenced and prosecuted in the small claims department if the amount or value claimed in the action does not exceed $10,000.

(4) Class actions may not be commenced and prosecuted in the small claims department.

(5) Actions providing for statutory attorney fees in which the amount or value claimed does not exceed $750 may be commenced and prosecuted in the small claims department or may be commenced and prosecuted in the regular department of the justice court. This subsection does not apply to an action based on contract for which attorney fees are authorized under ORS 20.082.

(6) Jurisdiction of the person of the defendant in an action commenced in the small claims department shall be deemed acquired as of the time of service of the notice and claim.

(7) Except as provided in ORS 55.065 (2)(c), the provisions of ORS 55.020 to 55.140 shall apply with regard to proceedings in the small claims department of any justice court.

(8) If a justice court is located in the same city as a circuit court, the justice court need not have a small claims department if the justice court and the circuit court enter into an intergovernmental agreement that provides that only the circuit court will operate a small claims department. If an intergovernmental agreement is entered into under this subsection, the agreement must establish appropriate procedures for referring small claims cases to the circuit court. [1963 c.404 §2 (enacted in lieu of 55.010); 1965 c.569 §2; 1973 c.625 §3; 1973 c.812 §7; 1975 c.346 §2a; 1975 c.592 §2; 1983 c.673 §6; 1985 c.367 §3; 1987 c.725 §3; 1989 c.583 §1; 1995 c.227 §4; 1997 c.801 §108; 1999 c.84 §5; 1999

c.673 §4; 2001 c.542 §6; 2007 c.125 §5; 2011 c.595 §53]

55.020 Commencement of action. An action in the small claims department shall be commenced by the plaintiff appearing in person or by agent or assignee before the court and filing a verified claim in the form prescribed by the justice of the peace along with the fee prescribed by ORS 51.310 (1)(c). [Amended by 1989 c.583 §2]

55.030 Contents of claim. The claim shall contain the name and address of the plaintiff and of the defendant, followed by a plain and simple statement of the claim, including the amount and date the claim allegedly accrued. The claim shall include an affidavit signed by the plaintiff and stating that the plaintiff made a bona fide effort to collect the claim from the defendant before filing the claim with the justice court. [Amended by 1977 c.875 §11; 1989 c.583 §3]

55.040 Verification and prosecution of claim. All claims shall be verified by the real party in interest, the agent or assignee of the party. Any claim may be filed and prosecuted in the small claims department by such agent or the assignee of the cause of action upon which recovery is sought.

55.045 Notice of claim; content; service. (1) Upon the filing of a claim, the court shall issue a notice in the form prescribed by the court.

(2) The notice shall be directed to the defendant, naming the defendant, and shall contain a copy of the claim.

(3) If the amount or value claimed is $50 or more, the notice and claim shall be served upon the defendant in the manner provided for the service of summons and complaint in proceedings in the circuit courts.

(4) If the amount or value claimed is less than $50, the notice and claim shall be served upon the defendant either in the manner provided for the service of summons and complaint in proceedings in the circuit courts or by certified mail, at the option of the plaintiff. If service by certified mail is attempted, the court shall mail the notice and claim by certified mail addressed to the defendant at the last-known mailing address of the defendant within the territorial jurisdiction of the court. The envelope shall be marked with the words "Deliver to Addressee Only" and "Return Receipt Requested." The date of delivery appearing on the return receipt shall be prima facie evidence of the date on which the notice and claim was served upon the defendant. If service

by certified mail is not successfully accomplished, the notice and claim shall be served in the manner provided for the service of summons and complaint in proceedings in the circuit courts.

(5) The notice shall include a statement in substantially the following form:

NOTICE TO DEFENDANT:
READ THESE PAPERS CAREFULLY!

Within 14 DAYS after receiving this notice you MUST do ONE of the following things:

Pay the claim plus fees and service expenses paid by plaintiff OR

Demand a hearing OR

Demand a jury trial

If you fail to do one of the above things within 14 DAYS after receiving this notice, then upon written request from the plaintiff, the court will enter a judgment against you for the amount claimed plus fees and service expenses paid by the plaintiff.

If you have questions about this notice, you should contact the court immediately.

[1989 c.583 §5]

55.050 [Amended by 1965 c.619 §28; 1977 c.875 §12; 1981 s.s. c.3 §95; 1987 c.829 §2; repealed by 1989 c.583 §11]

55.055 Explanation to plaintiff of how notice may be served. The justice of the peace shall provide to each plaintiff who files a claim with the small claims department of the court of the justice of the peace a written explanation of how notice may be served in actions in the department. [1977 c.875 §21]

55.065 Admission or denial of claim; request for jury trial. Within 14 days after the date of service of the notice and claim upon the defendant as provided in ORS 55.045:

(1) If the defendant admits the claim, the defendant may settle it by:

(a) Paying to the court the amount of the claim plus the amount of the small claims fee and service expenses paid by the plaintiff. The court shall pay to the plaintiff the amounts paid by the defendant.

(b) If the claim is for recovery of specific personal property, delivering the property to the plaintiff and paying to the plaintiff the amount of the small claims fee and service expenses paid by the plaintiff.

(2) If the defendant denies the claim, the defendant:

(a) May demand a hearing in the small claims department in a written request to the court in the form prescribed by the court, accompanied by payment of the defendant's fee prescribed; and

(b) When demanding a hearing, may assert a counterclaim in the form provided by the court; or

(c) If the amount or value claimed exceeds $750, may demand a jury trial in a written request to the court in the form prescribed by the court, accompanied by payment of the appearance fee prescribed by ORS 51.310 (1)(b) together with the trial fee prescribed by ORS 52.410. The request shall designate a mailing address to which a summons and copy of the complaint may be served by mail. Thereafter, the plaintiff's claim will not be limited to the amount stated in the claim, though it must involve the same controversy. [1989 c.583 §6; 1995 c.227 §3]

55.075 Time and place of hearing; procedure if right to jury trial asserted; fees. (1) If the defendant demands a hearing in the small claims department of the court, the court shall fix a day and time for the hearing and shall mail to the parties a notice of the hearing time in the form prescribed by the court, instructing them to bring witnesses, documents and other evidence pertinent to the controversy.

(2) If the defendant asserts a counterclaim, the notice of the hearing time shall contain a copy of the counterclaim.

(3) If the defendant claims the right to a jury trial, the court shall notify the plaintiff to file a formal complaint within 20 days following the mailing of such notice. The notice shall instruct the plaintiff to serve a summons and copy of the complaint by mail on the defendant at the designated address of the defendant. Proof of service of the summons and complaint copy may be made by certificate of the plaintiff or plaintiff's attorney attached to the complaint prior to its filing. The plaintiff's claim in such formal complaint is not limited to the amount stated in the claim filed in the small claims department but it must involve the same controversy. The defendant shall have 10 days in which to move, plead or otherwise appear following the day on which the summons and copy of the complaint would be delivered to the defendant in due course of mail. Thereafter, the cause shall proceed as other causes in the justice court,

and costs and disbursements shall be allowed and taxed and fees not previously paid shall be charged and collected as provided in ORS 51.310 and 52.410 for other cases tried in justice court, except that the appearance fee for plaintiff shall be an amount equal to the difference between the fee paid by the plaintiff as required by ORS 51.310 (1)(c) and the fee required of a plaintiff by ORS 51.310 (1)(a). [1989 c.583 §8]

55.077 Additional time for appearances; default and dismissal. (1) Upon written request, the court may extend to the parties additional time within which to make formal appearances required in the small claims department.

(2) If the defendant fails to pay the claim, demand a hearing or demand a jury trial, upon written request from the plaintiff, the court shall enter a judgment against the defendant for the relief claimed plus the amount of the small claims fee and service expenses paid by the plaintiff.

(3) If the plaintiff fails within the time provided to file a formal complaint pursuant to ORS 55.075 (3), the court shall:

(a) Dismiss the case without prejudice; and

(b) If the defendant applies therefor in writing to the court not later than 30 days after the expiration of the time provided for the plaintiff to file a formal complaint, refund to the defendant the amount of the jury trial fee paid by the defendant under ORS 55.065 (2)(c).

(4) If the defendant appears at the time set for hearing but no appearance is made by the plaintiff, the claim shall be dismissed with prejudice. If neither party appears, the claim shall be dismissed without prejudice.

(5) Upon good cause shown within 60 days, the court may set aside a default judgment or dismissal and reset the claim for hearing. [1989 c.583 §9]

55.080 Formal pleadings unnecessary; issuance of attachment, garnishment or execution; costs of execution taxable. No formal pleading, other than the claim and notice, shall be necessary. The hearing and disposition of all actions shall be informal, the sole object being to dispense justice between the litigants promptly. No attachment, garnishment or execution shall issue from the small claims department on any claim except as provided in this chapter. A prevailing party's costs in securing and service of such execution shall be taxed against the other party and recoverable as part of the judgment. [Amended by 1971 c.179 §1; 1977 c.875 §15]

55.090 Right of attorneys or persons not a party to appear; witnesses; disposition of controversy; appearance by attorney not required for any party. (1) Except as may otherwise be provided by ORS 55.040, no attorney at law nor any person other than the plaintiff and defendant shall become involved in or in any manner interfere with the prosecution or defense of the litigation in the department without the consent of the justice of the justice court, nor shall it be necessary to summon witnesses. But the plaintiff and defendant may offer evidence in their behalf by witnesses appearing at the hearing, and the justice may informally consult witnesses or otherwise investigate the controversy and give judgment or make such orders as the justice deems right, just and equitable for the disposition of the controversy.

(2) Notwithstanding ORS 9.320, a party that is not a natural person, state or any city, county, district or other political subdivision or public corporation in this state may appear as a party to any action in the department without appearance by attorney. [Amended by 1973 c.625 §4; 1987 c.158 §8; 1993 c.282 §3; 1997 c.808 §9; 2015 c.7 §4]

55.095 Counterclaim; procedure; fee; transfer of jurisdiction. (1) The defendant in an action in the small claims department may assert as a counterclaim any claim that, on the date of issuance of notice pursuant to ORS 55.045, the defendant may have against the plaintiff and that arises out of the same transaction or occurrence that is the subject matter of the claim filed by the plaintiff.

(2) If the amount of the counterclaim asserted by the defendant exceeds $10,000, the justice of the peace shall strike the counterclaim and proceed to hear and dispose of the case as though the counterclaim had not been asserted unless the defendant files with the counterclaim a motion requesting that the case be transferred from the small claims department to a court of appropriate jurisdiction and an amount to pay the costs of the transfer. After the transfer the plaintiff's claim will not be limited to the amount stated in the claim filed with the justice of the peace, though it must involve the same controversy.

(3)(a) If the amount or value of the counterclaim exceeds the jurisdictional limit of the justice court for a counterclaim and the defendant files a motion requesting transfer and an amount to pay the costs of transfer as provided in subsection (2) of this section, the case shall be transferred to the circuit court for the county in which the justice court is located and be governed as provided in ORS 52.320 for transfers to the circuit court. The justice court shall notify the plaintiff and defendant, by mail within 10 days following the order of transfer, of the transfer. The notice to the plaintiff shall contain a copy of the counterclaim and shall inform the plaintiff as to further pleading by the plaintiff in the court of appropriate jurisdiction.

(b) Upon filing the motion requesting transfer, the defendant shall pay to the court of appropriate jurisdiction an amount equal to the difference between the fee paid by the defendant as required by ORS 51.310 (1)(c) and the appearance fee for a defendant in the court of appropriate jurisdiction. [1977 c.875 §22; 1981 s.s. c.3 §96; 1983 c.673 §8; 1985 c.367 §4; 1987 c.725 §4; 1987 c.829 §3; 1989 c.583 §7; 1995 c.658 §65; 1997 c.801 §109; 1999 c.84 §6; 2007 c.125 §6; 2011 c.595 §53a]

55.100 Payment of judgment. If the judgment is against a party to make payment, the party shall pay the same forthwith upon the terms and conditions prescribed by the justice of the peace. [Amended by 1977 c.875 §16]

55.110 Conclusiveness of judgment; appeal; costs and fees on appeal. The judgment of the court shall be conclusive upon the plaintiff in respect to the claim filed by the plaintiff and upon the defendant in respect to a counterclaim asserted by the defendant. The defendant may appeal if dissatisfied in respect to the claim filed by the plaintiff. The plaintiff may appeal if dissatisfied in respect to a counterclaim asserted by the defendant. A party entitled to appeal may, within 10 days after the entry of the judgment against the party, appeal to the circuit court for the county in which the justice court is located. If final judgment is rendered against the party appealing in the appellate court, that party shall pay, in addition to the judgment, an attorney's fee to the other party in the sum of $10. Appeals from the small claims department shall only be allowed in cases in which appeals would be allowed if the action were instituted and the judgment rendered in the justice courts, as is provided by law. [Amended by 1977 c.875 §17; 1985 c.342 §10; 1995 c.658 §66]

55.120 Form of appeal; bond; proceedings in circuit court; no further appeal. (1) The appeal from the small claims department may be in the following form:

In the Circuit Court for _____ County, Oregon.

_____

Plaintiff,

vs.

_____

Defendant.

Comes now_____, a resident of _____ County, Oregon, and appeals from the decision of the small claims department of the justice court for _____ District, _____County, Oregon, wherein a judgment for _____ dollars was awarded against the appellant on the _____ day of_____, 2__.

_____, Appellant.

(2) All appeals shall be filed with the justice of the peace and accompanied by a bond, with satisfactory surety, to secure the payment of the judgment, costs and attorney's fees, as provided in ORS 55.110. The appeal shall be tried in the circuit court without any other pleadings than those required in the justice court originally trying the cause. All papers in the cause shall be certified to the circuit court as is provided by law in other cases of appeals in civil actions in justice courts. The circuit court may require any other or further statements or information it may deem necessary for a proper consideration of the controversy. The appeal shall be tried in the circuit court without a jury. There shall be no appeal from any judgment of the circuit court rendered upon the appeal, but such judgment shall be final and conclusive. [Amended by 1977 c.875 §18; 1985 c.342 §11; 2005 c.22 §38]

55.130 Enforcement of judgment when no appeal is taken; fees. (1) If no appeal is taken by a party against whom a judgment to make payment is rendered and the party fails to pay the judgment according to the terms and conditions thereof, the justice of the peace before whom the hearing was had, may, on application of the prevailing party, certify the judgment in substantially the following form:

In the Justice Court for _____ District, _____County, Oregon.

_____

Plaintiff,

vs.

_____

Defendant.

In the Small Claims Department

This is to certify that in a certain action before me, the undersigned, had on this, the _____ day of_____, 2__, wherein _____ was plaintiff and _____ was defendant, jurisdiction of the defendant having been had by personal service (or otherwise), as provided by law, I then and there entered judgment against the (defendant or plaintiff) in the sum of ___ dollars, which judgment has not been paid.

Witness my hand this ___ day of_____, 2__.

_____

Justice of the Peace
Sitting in the Small Claims Department.

---

(2) Upon the payment of a fee of $9, the justice of the peace shall forthwith enter the judgment transcript on the docket of the justice court. Thereafter execution and other process on execution provided by law may issue thereon as in other cases of judgments of justice courts, and transcripts of the judgments may be filed and entered in judgment dockets in circuit courts with like effect

as in other cases. [Amended by 1965 c.619 §30; 1977 c.875 §19; 1987 c.829 §4; 1997 c.801 §134; 2015 c.623 §5]

55.140 Separate docket for small claims department. Each justice of the peace shall keep a separate docket for the small claims department of the court of the justice of the peace, in which the justice of the peace shall make a permanent record of all proceedings, orders and judgments had and made in the small claims department.

CHAPTER 646—Unlawful Debt Collection Practices

2017 EDITION

646.639 Unlawful collection practices. (1) As used in subsection (2) of this section:

(a) "Consumer" means a natural person who purchases or acquires property, services or credit for personal, family or household purposes.

(b) "Consumer transaction" means a transaction between a consumer and a person who sells, leases or provides property, services or credit to consumers.

(c) "Commercial creditor" means a person who in the ordinary course of business engages in consumer transactions.

(d) "Credit" means the right granted by a creditor to a consumer to defer payment of a debt, to incur a debt and defer its payment, or to purchase or acquire property or services and defer payment therefor.

(e) "Debt" means any obligation or alleged obligation arising out of a consumer transaction.

(f) "Debtor" means a consumer who owes or allegedly owes an obligation arising out of a consumer transaction.

(g) "Debt collector" means any person who by any direct or indirect action, conduct or practice, enforces or attempts to enforce an obligation that is owed or due to any commercial creditor, or alleged to be owed or due to any commercial creditor, by a consumer as a result of a consumer transaction.

(h) "Person" means an individual, corporation, trust, partnership, incorporated or unincorporated association or any other legal entity.

(2) It shall be an unlawful collection practice for a debt collector, while collecting or attempting to collect a debt to do any of the following:

(a) Use or threaten the use of force or violence to cause physical harm to a debtor or to the debtor's family or property.

(b) Threaten arrest or criminal prosecution.

(c) Threaten the seizure, attachment or sale of a debtor's property when such action can only be taken pursuant to court order without disclosing that prior court proceedings are required.

(d) Use profane, obscene or abusive language in communicating with a debtor or the debtor's family.

(e) Communicate with the debtor or any member of the debtor's family repeatedly or continuously or at times known to be inconvenient to that person with intent to harass or annoy the debtor or any member of the debtor's family.

(f) Communicate or threaten to communicate with a debtor's employer concerning the nature or existence of the debt.

(g) Communicate without the debtor's permission or threaten to communicate with the debtor at the debtor's place of employment if the place is other than the debtor's residence, except that the debt collector may:

(A) Write to the debtor at the debtor's place of employment if no home address is reasonably available and if the envelope does not reveal that the communication is from a debt collector other than a provider of the goods, services or credit from which the debt arose.

(B) Telephone a debtor's place of employment without informing any other person of the nature of the call or identifying the caller as a debt collector but only if the debt collector in good faith has made an unsuccessful attempt to telephone the debtor at the debtor's residence during the day or during the evening between the hours of 6 p.m. and 9 p.m. The debt collector may not contact the debtor at the debtor's place of employment more frequently than once each business week and may not telephone the debtor at the debtor's place of employment if the debtor notifies the debt collector not to telephone at the debtor's place of employment or if the debt collector knows or has reason to know that the debtor's employer prohibits the debtor from receiving such communication. For the purposes of this subparagraph, any language in any instrument creating the debt which purports to authorize telephone calls at the debtor's place of employment shall not be considered as giving permission to the debt collector to call the debtor at the debtor's place of employment.

(h) Communicate with the debtor in writing without clearly identifying the name of the debt collector, the name of the person, if any, for whom the debt collector is attempting to collect the debt and the debt collector's business address, on all initial communications. In subsequent communications involving multiple accounts, the debt collector may eliminate the name of the person, if any, for whom the debt collector is attempting to collect the debt, and the term "various" may be substituted in its place.

(i) Communicate with the debtor orally without disclosing to the debtor within 30 seconds the name of the individual making the contact and the true purpose thereof.

(j) Cause any expense to the debtor in the form of long distance telephone calls, telegram fees or other charges incurred by a medium of communication, by concealing the true purpose of the debt collector's communication.

(k) Attempt to or threaten to enforce a right or remedy with knowledge or reason to know that the right or remedy does not exist, or threaten to take any action which the debt collector in the regular course of business does not take.

(l) Use any form of communication which simulates legal or judicial process or which gives the appearance of being authorized, issued or approved by a governmental agency, governmental official or an attorney at law when it is not in fact so approved or authorized.

(m) Represent that an existing debt may be increased by the addition of attorney fees, investigation fees or any other fees or charges when such fees or charges may not legally be added to the existing debt.

(n) Collect or attempt to collect any interest or any other charges or fees in excess of the actual debt unless they are expressly authorized by the agreement creating the debt or expressly allowed by law.

(o) Threaten to assign or sell the debtor's account with an attending misrepresentation or implication that the debtor would lose any defense to the debt or would be subjected to harsh, vindictive or abusive collection tactics.

(p) Use the seal or letterhead of a public official or a public agency, as those terms are defined in ORS 171.725.

(3) It shall be an unlawful collection practice for a debt collector, by use of any direct or indirect action, conduct or practice, to enforce or attempt to enforce an obligation made void and unenforceable by the provisions of ORS 759.720 (3) to (5). [1977 c.184 §2; 1985 c.799 §1; 1991 c.672 §9; 1991 c.906 §1; 1995 c.696 §50; 2013 c.551 §3]

APPENDIX B — RESOURCES

Below are some resources that *may* be available to you in preparing your case. The sooner you start your research and the sooner you contact potential sources of help, the better off you will be. Especially if you are looking for a free or low-cost lawyer to advocate for you, the "last minute" is a long time before the day of your hearing.

Books and other printed materials (some available at county law libraries)

Oregon State Bar legal publications (created for lawyers):

Construction Law
Contract Law in Oregon
Consumer Law in Oregon
Family Law
Insurance
Labor and Employment Law: Private Sector
Real Estate Disputes
Torts

Nolo self-help publications:

How to Win Your Personal Injury Claim
Everybody's Guide to Small Claims Court
Legal Research
Your Rights in the Workplace
Representing Yourself in Court

183

National Consumer Law Center publications:

> Surviving Debt
> Guide to the Rights of Utility Consumers
> Guide to Mobile Homes
> Student Loan Law

Legal Aid Services of Oregon self-help publications:

> Unpaid Consumer Bills
> Landlord-Tenant Law in Oregon

Internet resources

Oregon State Bar "For the Public"
www.osbar.org

Legal Aid Services of Oregon "Law Help"
www.oregonlawhelp.org

National Consumer Law Center
www.nclc.org

Nolo www.nolo.com

Student Loan Borrower Assistance Project
www.studentloanborrowerassistance.org

Note: It is rarely a good idea to purchase legal forms online. They seldom take into account state law and local procedures, and are usually a waste of your money.

Community mediation programs

Oregon Mediation Association—(503) 872-9775
https://law.uoregon.edu/explore/ADR-local-centers

Free legal aid programs for very low-income people

For the location of the office that serves your area, go to www.oregonlawhelp. org.

Law school legal clinic programs

Willamette University School of Law Clinics
Salem—(503) 370-6140

University of Oregon Law School Clinics
Eugene—contact Lane County Law and Advocacy Center

Private lawyers

Oregon State Bar Lawyer Referral Service—(800) 452-7636
Greatly reduced first consultation fee; reduced-fee representation for moderate- to low-income individuals in some kinds of cases

APPENDIX C — OREGON COURTS

Courthouse contact information

Be sure to ask when the court clerk's office is open to the public, too. Not every courthouse has the same hours.

CIRCUIT AND JUSTICE COURTS, by county

Baker County Courthouse (circuit and justice courts)
1995 Third Street, Suite 220
Baker City 97814
541-523-6305 (circuit court)
541-523-8213 (justice court)
> Huntington Justice Court
> 50 East Adams Street, P.O. Box 40
> Huntington 97907
> 541-869-2202

Benton County Courthouse
120 NW Fourth Street, P.O. Box 1870
Corvallis 97339
541-766-6859

Clackamas County Courthouse
807 Main Street
Oregon City 97045
503-655-8447

Clackamas County Justice Court
11750 SE 82nd Avenue, Suite D
Happy Valley 97086
503-794-3800

Clatsop County Courthouse
749 Commercial Street, P.O. Box 835
Astoria 97103
503-325-8555

Columbia County Courthouse (circuit and justice courts)
230 Strand Street
St. Helens 97051
503-397-2327 x0

Justice Court, Vernonia
1001 Bridge Street, P.O. Box 128
Vernonia 97064
503-429-2441

Coos County Courthouse—two locations
250 N Baxter Street
Coquille 97423
541-396-4100

North Bend Annex
1975 McPherson Avenue
North Bend 97459
541-756-2020

Crook County Courthouse
300 NE Third Street
Prineville 97754
541-447-6541

Curry County Courthouse
29821 Ellensburg Avenue
Mailing address: 94235 Moore Street, Suite 200
Gold Beach 97444
541-247-2511

Deschutes County Courthouse
1164 NW Bond Street
Bend 97703
541-388-5300

> Deschutes County Justice Court
> 2444 SW Glacier Place, P.O. Box 1750
> Redmond 97756
> 541-617-4758

Douglas County Justice Building
1036 SE Douglas Street, Room 201
Roseburg 97470
541-957-2471

> Canyonville Justice Court
> 249 NE Main Street, P.O. Box 376
> Canyonville 97417
> 541-839-4389

> Drain Justice Court
> 135 Second Street, P.O. Box 513
> Drain 97435
> 541-836-2814

> Glendale Justice Court
> 222 Gilbert Avenue, P.O. Box 325
> Glendale 97442
> 541-832-2101

Reedsport Justice Court
680 Fir Avenue
Reedsport 97467
541-271-4868

Gilliam County Courthouse (circuit and justice courts)
211 S Oregon Street
Condon 97823
541-384-3572

Arlington Justice Court
500 W First Street, P.O. Box 308
Arlington 97812
541-454-2923

Grant County Courthouse
201 S Humboldt Street, P.O. Box 159
Canyon City 97820
541-575-1438

Grant County Justice Court
201 S Humboldt Street, Suite 120
Canyon City 97820
541-575-1076

Harney County Courthouse
450 N Buena Vista Street, #16
Burns 97720
541-573-5207

Harney County Justice Court
450 N Buena Vista Street
Burns 97720
541-573-2346

Hood River County Courthouse
309 State Street
Hood River 97031
541-386-3535

Hood River County Justice Court
430 WaNaPa Street, P.O. Box 536
Cascade Locks 97014
541-374-8558

Jackson County Justice Building (circuit court)
100 S Oakdale Avenue
Medford 97501
541-776-7171 x 120

Jackson County Justice Court
505 Oak Street
Central Point 97502
541-774-1286

Jefferson County Courthouse
129 SW E Street, Suite 101
Madras 97741
541-475-3317

Josephine County Courthouse
500 NW Sixth Street
Grants Pass 97526
541-476-2309

Klamath County Courthouse
316 Main Street
Klamath Falls 97601
541-883-5503 x 0

Klamath County Justice Court
6500 S Sixth Street
Klamath Falls 97603
541-884-1864

Wood River Justice Court
212 First Street, P.O. Box 516
Chiloquin 97624
541-783-2240

Lake County Courthouse
523 Center Street
Lakeview 97630
541-947-6051

Lane County Courthouse
125 E Eighth Street
Eugene 97401
541-682-4020

Lane County Justice Court
900 Greenwood Street
Florence 97439
541-997-2535

Lincoln County Courthouse
225 W Olive Street
Newport 97365
541-265-4236

Linn County Courthouse
300 Fourth Avenue SW, P.O. Box 1749
Albany 97321
541-967-3802

Linn County Justice Court
430 Smith Street, P.O. Box 286
Harrisburg 97446
541-917-1903

Lebanon Justice Court
30 E Maple Street, #2
Lebanon 97355
541-258-5777

Sweet Home Justice Court
799 Long Street
Sweet Home 97386
541-367-5902

Malheur County Courthouse
251 B Street W
Vale 97918
541-473-5178

Malheur Justice Court
1178 SW Fourth Street, Apt 1
Ontario 97914
541-889-5712

Marion County Courthouse
100 High Street, P.O. Box 12869
Salem 97309
503-588-5105

East Marion Justice Court
111 W Locust Street, Suite 3
Stayton 97383
503-769-7656

North Marion Justice Court
986 N Pacific Highway
Woodburn 97071
503-981-8101

Morrow County Courthouse
100 Court Street, P.O. Box 609
Heppner 97836
541-676-5264

Heppner Justice Court
100 Court Street, P.O. Box 1125
Heppner 97836
541-676-9061

Irrigon Justice Court
205 Third Street at Main Street, P.O. Box 130
Irrigon 97841

Multnomah County Courthouse—two locations

1021 SW Fourth Street
Portland 97204
503-988-3957

East County Courthouse
18480 SE Stark Street
Gresham 97233
503-988-3957

Polk County Courthouse
850 Main Street
Dallas 97338
503-623-3154

Sherman County Courthouse
500 Court Street, P.O. Box 402
Moro 97039
541-565-3650

Sherman County Justice Court
500 Court Street, P.O. Box 282
Moro 97039
541-565-3572

Tillamook County Courthouse
201 Laurel Avenue
Tillamook 97141
503-842-2596 x 0

Tillamook County Justice Court
201 Laurel Avenue
Tillamook 97141
503-842-3416

Umatilla County Courthouse—two locations

216 SE Fourth Street
Pendleton 97801
541-278-0341 x 220

Stafford Hansel Government Center
915 SE Columbia Drive
Hermiston 97838
541-667-3020

Union County Courthouse
1105 K Avenue
La Grande 97850
541-962-9500 x 0

Union County Justice Court
10605 Island Avenue
Island City 97850
541-962-2997

Wallowa County Courthouse
101 South River Street
Enterprise 97828
541-426-4991

Wasco County Courthouse
511 Washington Street, P.O. Box 1400
The Dalles 97058
541-506-2700 x 0

Washington County Courthouse
145 N Second Avenue
Hillsboro 97124
503-846-8888

> Washington County Justice Court
> 3700 SW Murray Boulevard, Suite 150
> Beaverton 97005
> 503-846-6600

Wheeler County Courthouse
701 Adams Street, P.O. Box 308
Fossil 97830
541-763-2541

> Wheeler County Justice Court
> 701 Adams Street, P.O. Box 447
> Fossil 97830

> Wheeler County Justice Court
> 105 Nelson Street, P.O. Box 142

Mitchell 97750
541-462-3600

Yamhill County Courthouse
535 NE Fifth Street
McMinnville 97128
503-434-7530

GLOSSARY

actual damages—direct losses "out of pocket"--caused by wrongful conduct of another and claimed in a lawsuit

affidavit—a sworn statement signed before a notary public

affidavit of noncompliance—a sworn statement a party can file in some counties (see **SLR**, below) if the other party does not follow through on a mediated or stipulated judgment

answer—a court paper that a defendant files in court in response to a complaint or petition, to deny or challenge the claims of the plaintiff; in small claims court an answer is called **defendant's notice of election**

appellant—a person who appeals a judge's decision in justice court to circuit court

appellee—the winner of a case in justice court against whom the other party appeals to circuit court

arbitration—a formal meeting of the parties to a dispute before someone serving as a judge, where that person hears the facts and the law and makes a decision that may or may not be binding on the parties.

assign—give or sell an interest or a right to a person or entity that then can enforce the right

assumed business name—a name used for business that is not the owner's name

attachment—after a judgment for money, the process used by the judgment creditor to get payment

bond—money or a type of insurance to guarantee to the court that a party will pay for the other side's likely costs if the party loses the case

capacity, legal capacity—the ability to care for one's own safety and well-being. See 'guardian'

circuit court—in Oregon, a court of general jurisdiction; a court with the authority to hear all kinds of state-law and some kinds of federal-law cases

civil case—a case involving claims of unlawful conduct by individuals or entities, in which the state does not prosecute a defendant for a crime. Crime includes traffic citations and other minor crimes for which the defendant has received a "ticket."

claim—the basis for filing a court case; also, the form used to start a case in small claims court. The claim form is sometimes called a **complaint**.

claim of exemption—an objection filed by a judgment debtor to an attempt by a judgment creditor to take money or belongings of the debtor when the debtor believes that those things cannot lawfully be taken. See **exempt property.**

class action—a type of lawsuit in which one or more individuals act on behalf of a large group of persons

conservator—a person who is legally authorized to handle the financial affairs of someone who lacks capacity to make financial decisions

contest; contested—file an answer in a case, challenging plaintiff's claim about certain facts or about applicable law; a contested case is one in which the defendant has filed an answer, with the result that the case will head toward trial

continue, continuance—postpone, postponement of trial

contract—a legally binding agreement

costs, also called court costs--the costs of filing or responding to a claim, of serving the other parties, etc. The court awards the right to the prevailing party in a case to collect costs from the losing party.

counterclaim—a claim raised by a defendant against the plaintiff in a civil case, where the claim is related to a claim raised by the plaintiff against the defendant

creditor—a person or an entity to whom a debtor owes money

damages—a general term that covers a variety of losses claimed by a plaintiff (or counterclaimant) in a lawsuit, and which may include actual damages, statutory damages, liquidated damages, and punitive damages

debtor's examination—after a creditor obtains a money judgment against a debtor, a court proceeding at which the debtor is forced to appear and to provide information about all of his or her assets, resources, and income

declaration—a statement made under penalty of perjury but not witnessed by a notary

default—in a lawsuit, default occurs when a defendant does not file an answer or motion within the required time limit to respond to a complaint filed against him or her; plaintiff will get what he or she asked for in the complaint without further court proceedings or notice to defendant

defendant—a person or entity that is sued by a plaintiff

defendant's notice of election—in small claims court, this is the defendant's answer to the plaintiff's claims, and describes whether the defendant is going to fight those claims, whether defendant wants a jury trial, and has any counterclaims

defense—a legal position taken by a defendant that keeps a plaintiff from winning a case

demand letter—a letter to a potential defendant asking for payment, property, or a change in conduct in order to prevent a lawsuit

dismissal—action the court takes to "throw out" a case, usually without making a decision about the facts and law in the case. See also **prejudice**.

element—a type of fact that a party must prove in a particular case. In a criminal homicide case, for example, the prosecutor must prove these elements: a person (1) intentionally (2) killed (3) another person (4) without any justification. Every type of legal claim has its own specific elements.

exempt property—specific amounts of money and other property that a non-government judgment creditor cannot lawfully take from a judgment debtor

exhibit—an item that a party offers as evidence during a trial

expert witness—someone who testifies about a technical aspect of evidence to help the judge understand facts that are important--such as the reactions of fabrics to certain chemicals during dry cleaning, the correct diagnosis of a car problem, what building standards apply to home improvements and the quality of those improvements, or the likely speed of a car based on the length of skid marks on the road, etc. An expert witness testifies on the basis of his or her advanced training, education, skill, or experience. The expert does not have to personally witness facts and events on which a case is based.

fee deferral—an order of a court to permit a party to file a complaint or respond to a complaint without having to pay the full court filing fee at the time of filing

fee waiver—an order of a court to permit a party to file a complaint or respond to a complaint without having to pay a court filing fee

filing fee—the cost to a party to start a court case or a submit a response to a case that another party has started

forfeiture—a legal action that gives someone the right to take away someone's property, such as the forfeiture of land or cars used in illegal drug manufacture, or a right under a contract to take back items not fully paid for after getting a court order to do so

garnishee—a third person (such as a bank or an employer) with control over money that belongs to a judgment creditor; a garnishee has the duty to turn over some or all of the funds in response to a garnishment

garnishment—a legal process that allows a judgment creditor to collect a debt by taking funds from a worker's paycheck, a business's proceeds, or a bank account; it is a type of attachment

guardian—a person who is legally responsible for another person who lacks the mental or physical capacity to make decisions affecting his or her health, safety, or well-being

guardian ad litem—an adult who appears in court on behalf of a minor

injunction, injunctive relief—a judgment by a court ordering a person or an entity to stop conduct that is harmful to another

judgment—the final decision in a court case, made by a judge

judgment creditor—a person or entity that has obtained a court decision giving the creditor the right to force payment of a debt owed to the creditor

judgment debtor—a person or entity against whom another party has the right under a court order to force payment of a debt

judgment lien—a lien on property that is created by a court judgment against the owner of the property

judgment-proof—the financial status of a person that is so low that the person has nothing that a judgment creditor can lawfully take

jurisdiction—authority of a court or type of court to hear certain kinds of cases in a specific geographic area

justice court—a type of court in some Oregon counties that has jurisdiction over traffic offenses and other minor citations, rental evictions, and small claims

lien—a right to part of the value of the property of another that the law will enforce

liquidated damages—an amount of money awarded in a case in which it is difficult to determine a party's actual damages; can be authorized by statute or contract

mechanic's lien—the right of an auto mechanic to keep someone's vehicle until the owner pays the mechanic for work done on the vehicle

mediation—a process outside of court (although it may be connected to the court system) in which a trained facilitator works with parties to resolve their dispute among themselves instead of giving control over the decision to a judge

motion—a formal request to a court to take action or to allow a party to take action within an ongoing case; motions are often in writing

move—ask the court for something; file a motion to ask the court for something

negligence—a basis on which to sue a defendant for damages. The plaintiff must show the court that the defendant had a duty to exercise reasonable care toward the plaintiff, the defendant breached that duty, and that the defendant's misconduct caused harm to the plaintiff

notice of claim—in small claims court, official notice to a defendant that a claim has been filed against her or him

notice of election—see defendant's notice of election

ORCP, Oregon Rules of Civil Procedure—a collection of court rules that describes the "how to" of conducting the various steps of a case. Not all of the ORCP apply to small claims court, but many judges refer to them for guidance in small claims matters.

ORS—Oregon Revised Statutes, the state laws that apply in Oregon

party—a person or entity that is a plaintiff or a defendant in a lawsuit

penalty—a fee allowed by contract or statute for certain actions, such as failure to complete a contract project on time, intentionally passing a bad check, etc

plaintiff—a person or entity that starts a lawsuit against someone else

post-judgment interest—the amount of interest (9% simple) a court will apply to a money award in a judgment if there is no written contract between the parties that requires a different amount

prejudice—to have an effect on a party's rights. A court can dismiss a claim **with prejudice** (barring the party from coming to court again on the same claim) or **without prejudice** (allowing the party to come to court with the same case later on)

preponderance of the evidence—the "standard" of evidence by which a plaintiff must prove a claim in most civil cases; that is, the plaintiff must show that, more likely than not, the harm complained of did occur and that the defendant is at fault

prevailing party—the party that wins a lawsuit; it can be either the plaintiff or the defendant

prevailing party fee—a fee the court awards from the loser to the winner of a case to compensate the winner for the time and expense involved in preparing for the case; the fee is in addition to court costs

private attorney general—a person who files a lawsuit to protect certain rights of the general public (such as rental housing or environmental safety), when a statute allows

pro bono—short for "pro bono publico," or for the public good, referring to an attorney's representing a party without charging a fee

process server—a mentally competent person over the age of 18 who personally delivers or mails court summonses and other court notices; the term includes sheriffs and other law enforcement; professional servers; and volunteers

pro tem judge—someone who is not a regular judge

punitive damages—money damages in addition to other damages that a court may sometimes award when the behavior of one of the parties has been not only unlawful but deliberate and outrageous; to punish the wrongdoer and dis- courage similar behavior in the future

real party in interest—the person or entity whose rights are affected by a lawsuit

rebuttal—a party's opportunity to disprove any claims raised by the other party after the other party has presented his or her side of the case

recusal (recuse)—occurs when a judge has or is believed to have personal interests or biases that make it difficult for the judge to be impartial in a specific case

replevin—a case in which the plaintiff (or counter claimant) seeks the return of personal property

return of service—a document signed by a process server to inform the court he or she succeeded in finding defendants and giving them a plaintiff's complaint

server—a process server

service, or service of process—the act of delivering or sending court summonses to the defendants in a case

set aside default, motion to—request by a party to re-start a case after the other party won the case by obtaining a default judgment when the first party did not file an answer or did not appear at the trial

statute—law passed by a legislature; in Oregon, the Oregon Revised Statutes are laws enacted by the legislature

statute of limitations—the time limit in which a person or entity has the right to sue a defendant on a particular matter

statutory attorney fees—fees an attorney for the prevailing party in a case is entitled to collect from the losing party in the case, as permitted by the statutes on which the case is based—such as in consumer and landlord-tenant cases

statutory damages—a range or set amount of money that a law says someone is entitled to if the person wins a lawsuit; the amount can be instead of other damages or in addition to them, depending on statute

stipulated judgment—an agreement signed by all the parties to a case, accepted by the judge as the order of the court

summons—the official notice to a defendant that a lawsuit has been filed against her or him. In small claims court, the summons is part of the same form as the claim, and is called a **notice of claim**

Supplemental Local Rules (SLR)—procedures required by local courts, in addition to rules applied generally by the UTCR. SLRs differ from county to county; not all counties have them.

testimony—statements made under oath about facts in a case

tort—wrongful conduct that results in harm to a person or entity and that can be the basis for a claim in a civil case (for example, damage caused by a reckless driver, harm to a tenant or a tenant's friend by a dangerous condition the landlord should have fixed, race discrimination in housing or employment, etc). Tortious conduct can be intentional or negligent. In the case of certain consumer products, making a defective product can be a tort.

uncontested—a case in which the defendant has not filed an answer or motion to challenge the claims of the plaintiff. In an uncontested case, the plaintiff should generally get what he or she asked for from the court.

Uniform Trial Court Rules (UTCR)—general rules that apply to procedures used in most courts in Oregon

venue—the county in which a plaintiff is allowed to file a case

with prejudice—with respect to a court decision in a case, a ruling that decides the outcome of a case so that the plaintiff is not free to file the same case again

without prejudice—with respect to a court decision, usually a dismissal of a case without barring plaintiff from filing the same case later

witness—a person who testifies in court about facts of which she or he has personal knowledge (from seeing or hearing, etc) ; see also 'expert witness'

writ of attachment—a court order to a sheriff to collect property from a judgment debtor

writ of execution—a court order to a sheriff to collect money from a judgment debtor

writ of garnishment—a court order to a garnishee, requiring that person or entity to turn over to the judgment creditor money it holds for the debtor

INDEX

www.ingramcontent.com/pod-product-compliance
Lightning Source LLC
Chambersburg PA
CBHW051344200326
41521CB00014B/2476